STONEWALL KITCHEN
BREAKFAST

STONEWALL KITCHEN
BREAKFAST

A Collection of Great Morning Meals

BY JONATHAN KING, JIM STOTT & KATHY GUNST

Photographs by Jim Stott

CHRONICLE BOOKS

SAN FRANCISCO

Library of Congress Cataloging-in-Publication Data available.

ISBN 978-0-8118-6867-9

Manufactured in China.

Designed by Katie Heit
Prop styling by Andrea Kuhn
Food styling by Catrine Kelty

10 9 8 7 6 5 4 3 2 1

Chronicle Books LLC
680 Second Street
San Francisco, California 94107

www.chroniclebooks.com

P. 47: Huevos Rancheros from *Stonewall Kitchen Favorites* by
Jonathan King, Jim Stott, and Kathy Gunst. Used by permission
of Random House, Inc.

DEDICATION

To our family and friends and the wonderful guests of Stonewall Kitchen who have supported us from our beginnings—even in the rain at the local farmers' market
—J.K. and J.S.

To John, Maya, and Emma
—K.G.

ACKNOWLEDGMENTS

Many thanks to our editor, Amy Treadwell, for her insights on this project. To Peter Perez, for helping shepherd the project along, and to Katie Heit, for her gorgeous book design. Thanks to Doug Ogan, David Hawk, Ben Kasman, and everyone at Chronicle Books who helped make the book happen.

To Doe Coover, our agent, for her vision and enthusiasm.

Thanks to the amazingly talented photo team for making every image so beautiful: Andrea Kuhn, prop stylist; Catrine Kelty, food stylist; John McNeil, photo assistant, and Kim Gallagher, kitchen assistant.

Many thanks to Hope Murphy for helping test the recipes.

TABLE OF CONTENTS

CHAPTER 6
Pancakes, French Toast & Waffles

CHAPTER 7
Side Dishes

CHAPTER 8
Drinks

*This symbol indicates a dish that is **quick and simple** and perfect for a weekday morning when you're running late, trying to eat something good, and make it out of the house in minutes. This symbol might also indicate that the dish can be made ahead and simply reheated quickly in the morning.*

INTRODUCTION

How do you start your day? Walk the dog, feed the baby, and drive the kids to school? Or do you go to the gym and work out, take a walk in the woods, or weed the garden? What you do first thing each day says a lot about who you are. What you eat first thing in the morning offers even more insight about your true nature. Breakfast may be the most personal meal of the day.

Are you the type who takes good care of yourself and makes sure to eat breakfast every morning—something healthful and quick like a fruit smoothie, a bowl of whole-grain cereal, or a granola bar? Or do you grab a bagel and cream cheese and a cup of java from the nearest coffee shop? Perhaps you're in for a really long, hard day and you need more sustenance with a full "American" breakfast—fried eggs, bacon, home fries, toast, jelly, orange juice, and coffee? Or is the morning meal a celebration of sorts? Will you cook pancakes or waffles, an oven-baked frittata, fresh-from-the-oven muffins, and put together a special fruit salad? Will you spend several leisurely hours with the morning paper, a mug of fresh-brewed tea, and let the meal—and the day— evolve gently?

While there are a lot of choices, Americans tend to have fairly limited ideas about what kind of food passes for breakfast. But breakfast can be quite different in other parts of the world. A traditional Chinese breakfast often includes a kind of rice porridge called *congee*, steamed dumplings, and a savory soy milk drink. In Mexico and other parts of Latin America, eggs are fried and served with black or red beans, warm tortillas, spicy salsa, and guacamole. A traditional Japanese breakfast includes miso soup instead of coffee; and in England the morning meal can include toast, eggs, bacon, sausage, and kippers or smoked fish—and, of course, a pot of good, strong tea. Mediterranean countries enjoy fruit, yogurt, whole-grain cereals, olives, tomatoes, cucumbers, ham, cheeses, and crusty breads (always with very strong coffee). In France the tradition of dipping buttery croissants into steaming cups of frothy milk-topped *café au lait* still reigns. And in Spain, fresh-grated tomatoes are spooned onto crusty bread toasted with olive oil and, sometimes, a touch of garlic.

What can be said about the first meal of the day here? Speed seems to be

"...ON A BUSY WORKDAY, PRESSED FOR TIME, AND RUNNING LATE AS USUAL, I ASSEMBLE A YOGURT PARFAIT: FRESH VANILLA YOGURT TOPPED WITH STONEWALL'S HOMEMADE GRANOLA."

the defining element in the American breakfast—grabbing a doughnut and coffee, breakfast sandwich, or granola bar—on the way to work or school in the car, on the subway, or on the bus while we run, run, run. However, on weekends we do like to slow down and enjoy more elaborate morning meals. In the South, grits are still a part of traditional breakfasts. Residents of New Orleans prefer dipping beignets (deep-fried fritters coated in powdered sugar) into their chicory coffee. In the Rockies (where beef is king), you'll find thick breakfast steaks served with fried eggs and toast. But, in California, home to the super-health-conscious,

many omelets (whites only, of course) include avocado. And in parts of northern New England, diners serve baked beans and fish chowder with the morning eggs and hearty pancakes with local maple syrup.

The three of us also have different takes on the morning meal. When we got together to talk about a book devoted to breakfast, there were many stories that spilled forth.

Jonathan states: "My favorite breakfast memories were those crazy unexpected times when my mom announced we were having 'breakfast night.' We would run full blast upstairs and put on our zip-up pajamas—with the feet cut off to handle the current growth spurt. Mom would usually make French toast served with warmed maple syrup and crisp bacon. All six kids would sit around the crowded table eating off unmatched plates, grinning ear to ear, anxiously awaiting Mom serving the next hot French toast perfectly balanced on her ancient spatula, directly out of the fry pan. It's funny—I look back and realize Mom was brilliant; it was the only time we wouldn't fuss about getting ready for bed.

"Now, on a busy workday, pressed for time, and running late as usual, I assemble a yogurt parfait: fresh vanilla yogurt topped with Stonewall's homemade granola. Sometimes I'll stir a teaspoon or two of wild blueberry jam into the yogurt. If I have a bit more time, I love simple egg

sandwiches, my favorite being scrambled eggs tossed with cheese and herbs, topped with salsa and rolled up in a tortilla wrap.

"I've never understood people who don't eat breakfast. To me it's like saying you don't breathe all day. I love breakfast and much of our company is based on the morning meal. Our farmhouse pancake and waffle mixes, marmalades, fruit curds, spreads, jams, and syrups are all inspired from our love of this treasured meal."

"Some folks need a little space and a lot of coffee to wake up," says Jim. "Not me. I wake about six-ish with a burst of energy and a huge appetite. I'm a man with a mission in the morning and our youngest dog, Violet, is right on the same page with me. I don't know if she has trained me, or if my morning ritual has

influenced her, but as soon as my feet touch the floor she is up and running to the kitchen. When I arrive she is sitting next to the counter, by her cookie jar, tail wagging, and with the sweetest look on her face.

"My favorite mornings are when we don't have a tight schedule, because I get a thrill out of making breakfast and serving it in bed. It could be the best way I know to say 'I love you' without uttering a word.

"My mom always made us a great breakfast: bacon and eggs, French toast, creamy old-fashioned oatmeal with brown sugar and raisins, or her delicious hash with poached eggs. Some Sundays we would wake to the smell of my dad making homemade doughnuts—nothing was better."

"MY FAVORITE MORNINGS ARE WHEN WE DON'T HAVE A TIGHT SCHEDULE, BECAUSE I GET A THRILL OUT OF MAKING BREAKFAST AND SERVING IT IN BED. IT COULD BE THE BEST WAY I KNOW TO SAY 'I LOVE YOU' WITHOUT UTTERING A WORD."

"We grew up eating the latest, greatest, sugar-packed cereal," recalls Kathy. "Our pantry was lined with boxes of bright pinks, oranges, and greens—not a whole grain in sight. The big treat was Sunday morning when my dad would take over the kitchen. You need to understand that, when I was growing up in the '60s, my father wasn't the sort to spend time in the kitchen. Other than manning the barbecue on summer weekends, the cooking was my mother's territory. But on Sunday mornings, my father would scramble eggs, crisp up the bacon, and pop the English muffins into the toaster and pretend he was a short-order cook. When we were little, my brothers and I would laugh uncontrollably at the sight of our father, wearing my mother's apron tied around his thick waist, screaming, 'Who's got two over easy? I said two over easy with toast and bacon!'

"Writing a book about breakfast was nothing short of a revelation for me. I was never much of a breakfast eater. Of course I have spent years listening to nutritionists talk about how breakfast is 'the best way get a healthy start to the day.' But lunch and dinner and late-night snacks always struck me as *so* much more interesting. A good cup of strong espresso with steamed milk, a slice of French bread, and maybe a banana were the most I could muster interest in before noon.

"But then I started cooking and testing and experimenting with breakfast recipes. It sounds like an exaggeration to call myself a 'convert,' but I think I am. I just can't imagine not eating a morning meal now."

Stonewall Kitchen Breakfast addresses all types of morning people just like us. We've got a fabulous granola (page 38) and granola bar (page 40) for those who can't be bothered doing much more than grabbing a bowl, the milk, and a spoon. For the health nut we have an assortment of fruit smoothies (page 33) that can be thrown into a blender and whirled up in a matter of minutes (less time than it takes to open the paper and make a cup of coffee). And then we get a bit more serious.

For those who crave a morning meal but have less than fifteen minutes to prepare it (the speed freaks), we have all kinds of muffins, fruit butters, flavored cream cheeses, and breakfast sandwiches that can be made the night before, or assembled in no time at all. These ideas range from a Spanish-style tomato toast (topped with grated tomatoes, cheese, and fresh basil leaves, then placed under the broiler for two minutes; page 75) to a fabulous sandwich we call a B.E.L.T (page 79). If you thought BLTs were good, wait until you try our Bacon, Egg, Lettuce, and Tomato sandwich! You can also make an open-faced egg sandwich (thin slices of hard-boiled eggs on whole-wheat toast) flavored with a saffron-rosemary spread

and sweet, crunchy pequillo peppers (full of vitamin C; page 76). Or try a batch of our Peach, Sour Cream, and Crystallized Ginger Muffins (page 19) with Peach-Ginger Butter (page 128) or our Carrot Cake Muffins with Cream Cheese–Walnut Spread (page 17). Grab a muffin (you can make them weeks ahead and freeze them), a cup of coffee, and you're ready to go!

Even though we live in a gotta-hurry-up-or-I'll-be-late kind of world, there is a time and place for breakfast to be leisurely and celebratory. We have plenty of ideas for weekend brunches, holiday mornings, and that rare day when you don't have to run. Smoked Salmon and Arugula Benedict with Arugula-Lemon Butter (page 68) or Lobster Benedict with Meyer Lemon–Scallion Butter (page 65) are both dishes full of bright, fresh

flavors that set a festive mood. Or there's Huevos Rancheros (page 47), Chorizo Hash (page 123), and an amazing Breakfast Pizza (page 84)—that's right, with fried eggs, bacon, and cheese on a store-bought crust—that might make you rethink pizza altogether.

Here's to the morning and all the possibilities it holds for each and every one of us. Here's to the first meal of the day. Make it a good one.

—Jonathan King, Jim Stott, and Kathy Gunst

CHAPTER

MUFFINS, SCONES

&

COFFEE CAKE

CARROT CAKE MUFFINS WITH CREAM CHEESE–WALNUT SPREAD

MAKES 16 MUFFINS | QUICK AND SIMPLE 🕐

Imagine a muffin with all the moistness and flavor of a carrot cake but one that can be made from start to finish in well under an hour. Grated carrots, unsweetened coconut, walnuts, and spices combine in these muffins to make a delicious morning treat. The muffins can be served hot or at room temperature with a simple cream cheese and walnut mixture instead of butter. Make the muffins the night ahead for a quick breakfast.

The inspiration for this recipe came from Dorie Greenspan's Carrot Spice Muffins from her book *Baking*.

INGREDIENTS

THE MUFFIN BATTER

Vegetable spray for the muffin pans

2 cups all-purpose flour

½ cup packed light brown sugar

⅓ cup granulated sugar

2 teaspoons baking powder

1½ teaspoons ground cinnamon

½ teaspoon baking soda

½ teaspoon ground allspice

½ teaspoon ground ginger

¼ teaspoon salt

2 large eggs

⅔ cup canola oil

⅔ cup low-fat milk

½ teaspoon vanilla extract

1 cup packed grated peeled carrots (about 2 large)

⅔ cup grated unsweetened coconut

½ cup (2 ounces) chopped walnuts, almonds, or pecans (see Note)

: : : : :

THE CREAM CHEESE–WALNUT SPREAD

1 cup cream cheese, at room temperature

½ cup (2 ounces) chopped walnuts, almonds, or pecans (see Note)

1. Place a rack in the middle of the oven and preheat it to 375 degrees F.

2. *Make the muffins:* Lightly coat 16 muffin cups with the vegetable spray.

3. In a large bowl, whisk together the flour, brown sugar, granulated sugar, baking powder, cinnamon, baking soda, allspice, ginger, and salt.

4. In a medium bowl, whisk together the eggs. Whisk in the oil, milk, and vanilla until well mixed. Pour the oil/egg

Continued…

...continued

mixture into the flour mixture and mix gently. Add the carrots, coconut, and walnuts and mix until just incorporated. Divide the batter among the prepared muffin cups, filling each one about halfway.

5. Bake for 18 to 22 minutes, or until the tops of the muffins are pale golden brown and a toothpick inserted in the center comes out clean.

Remove from the oven and let cool in the pans for a few minutes. Using a table knife, gently lift the muffins out of their cups and place them on a cooling rack.

6. *Make the spread:* In a small bowl, using a soft spatula, mix together the cream cheese and the nuts. Serve the spread on the side or on top of the warm muffins.

NOTE

For a nuttier flavor, lightly toast the nuts on a cookie sheet in a 350 degree F oven for about 10 minutes, or until lightly browned. Cool and chop.

BIGGER, BETTER MUFFINS

HELPFUL HINTS

Any of the muffin recipes in this book can be made in larger 6-muffin pans instead of the regular 12-muffin pans. Divide the batter among the 6-muffin cups and bake for 5 to 10 minutes longer, or until a toothpick inserted in the center of a muffin comes out clean.

PEACH, SOUR CREAM, AND CRYSTALLIZED GINGER MUFFINS

MAKES 12 MUFFINS | QUICK AND SIMPLE 🕐

We love making these muffins in the late summer when peaches are fresh, ripe, and dripping with sweet juice. But they also work well year-round using frozen peaches. Serve with Peach-Ginger Butter (page 128).

INGREDIENTS

Vegetable spray for the muffin pans

2 cups all-purpose flour

2 teaspoons baking powder

½ teaspoon baking soda

Pinch of salt

1 stick (½ cup) unsalted butter, at room temperature

⅔ cup sugar

2 large eggs

¼ teaspoon vanilla extract

¾ cup sour cream

1½ cups peeled and chopped fresh or frozen peaches

¼ cup finely chopped crystallized ginger

1. Place a rack in the middle of the oven and preheat it to 400 degrees F.

2. Lightly coat 12 muffin cups with the vegetable spray.

3. In a large bowl, whisk together the flour, baking powder, baking soda, and salt.

4. Beat the butter in a stand mixer with the paddle attachment or using a hand-held mixer on medium speed, until creamy. Add the sugar and beat for about 4 minutes, until light and fluffy. Add the eggs one at a time on low speed, using a spatula to scrape down the sides of the bowl. Add the vanilla and mix to combine.

5. Add half of the flour mixture and mix on low until blended. Add the sour cream

and mix until combined. Add the remaining flour mixture and mix until just combined. Remove the bowl from the mixer and, using a soft spatula, gently stir in the peaches and ginger, making sure they are well distributed in the batter.

6. Divide the batter between the prepared muffin cups, filling each one almost full. Bake for 20 to 25 minutes, or until the tops of the muffins are golden brown and a toothpick inserted in the center comes out clean. Cool the muffins in the pan for about 5 minutes and then, using a table knife, gently lift the muffins out of their cups and place them on a cooling rack. Serve warm or at room temperature.

BASIL AND GOAT CHEESE MUFFINS

MAKES 12 MUFFINS | QUICK AND SIMPLE 🕐

Muffins don't need to be sweet. These are filled with tangy goat cheese, flecked with fresh basil, thyme, and lemon zest, and are delicious served hot with a simple Lemon-Herb Butter.

INGREDIENTS

Vegetable spray for the muffin pans

1½ cups all-purpose flour

1 tablespoon baking powder

Salt

1 cup milk

¾ stick (6 tablespoons) unsalted butter, melted

1 large egg

Freshly ground black pepper

4 ounces soft goat cheese, well chilled and crumbled

2 tablespoons thinly sliced fresh basil

1 tablespoon chopped fresh thyme

1 teaspoon grated lemon zest

Lemon-Herb Butter (page 127)

1. Place a rack in the middle of the oven and preheat it to 375 degrees F.

2. Lightly coat 12 muffin cups with the vegetable spray.

3. Sift the flour, baking powder, and ⅛ teaspoon of salt into a bowl. In a large bowl, whisk together the milk, butter, egg, a tiny dash of salt, and a generous grinding of pepper. Add the flour mixture and stir until just incorporated.

4. In a small bowl, mix together the goat cheese, basil, thyme, lemon zest, and a generous grinding of pepper. Add 1 tablespoon of the cheese mixture to the muffin batter and mix to combine.

5. Fill the prepared muffin cups almost halfway with the batter. Divide the goat cheese mixture among the muffin cups. Top with the remaining batter.

6. Bake for 25 minutes, or until the tops of the muffins are a pale golden brown and a toothpick inserted in the center comes out clean (if there's goat cheese on the toothpick, that's fine). Let cool for 1 or 2 minutes in the pan and then, using a table knife, gently lift the muffins out of their cups and place them on a cooling rack. Serve warm with the Lemon-Herb Butter.

APPLE AND APRICOT BUTTERMILK SCONES WITH MAPLE-ALMOND GLAZE

MAKES 12 SCONES | QUICK AND SIMPLE ⏱

If you think scones are supposed to be dry and crumbly (read: boring), think again. These pastries are light, fluffy in texture, and chock-full of the flavor of fresh apples and sweet dried apricots. When the scones are almost done baking, you brush them with maple syrup and press slivered almonds on top for a sweet, simple glaze. They are excellent served with lemon curd.

INGREDIENTS

3 cups all-purpose flour

⅓ cup sugar

2½ teaspoons baking powder

¾ teaspoon salt

½ teaspoon baking soda

1½ sticks (¾ cup) unsalted butter, well chilled and diced

¾ cup dried apricots, cut into ⅛-inch pieces, or raisins or currants

1 large crisp apple, such as Macoun or McIntosh, peeled and cut into ½-inch cubes

½ teaspoon ground cinnamon

1 cup buttermilk

About 1 cup maple syrup

About 1 cup (4 ounces) slivered almonds

1. Place a rack in the middle of the oven and preheat it to 400 degrees F.

2. In the container of a food processor, pulse the flour, sugar, baking powder, salt, and baking soda. Add the chilled butter and pulse until the butter becomes pea sized. Transfer the flour mixture to a large bowl and add the apricots, apple, and cinnamon. Gently toss to coat with flour.

3. Make a well in the middle of the flour mixture and pour in the buttermilk. Gradually push the flour into the buttermilk and start to gently mix until the sides of the bowl become clean.

4. Separate the dough into 2 pieces and gently shape each piece into a disk about 7 inches in diameter and 1½ inches thick. Cut each disk into 6 wedges and place each wedge on a greased cookie sheet, making sure to space them at least 1 inch apart.

5. Bake for about 20 minutes, or until a pale golden brown on top. Remove from the oven. Using a pastry brush or the back of a spoon, generously brush each scone with the maple syrup and press a generous tablespoon of the almonds on top. Bake for another 5 to 8 minutes, or until lightly browned. Transfer to a rack to cool.

VARIATIONS

Substitute a pear for the apple and add ⅓ cup chopped crystallized ginger in addition to the raisins.

Add ¼ teaspoon ground all-spice or ginger to the mixture.

Add ½ cup slivered almonds to the batter with the fruit.

COFFEE CAKE BUTTERMILK MUFFINS

MAKES 12 MUFFINS | QUICK AND SIMPLE 🕐

We set out to create a quick, easy muffin that has all the appeal—not to mention the flavors and texture—of a great coffee cake. A simple muffin batter is made with buttermilk and a touch of cinnamon and then layered with a coffee cake swirl of chopped walnuts, sugar, and cinnamon. The muffins are moist and so chock-full of spice and nuts that they don't need butter. Serve warm or at room temperature.

INGREDIENTS

THE COFFEE CAKE SWIRL
¾ cup (2 ounces) coarsely chopped walnuts

⅓ cup sugar

1½ teaspoons ground cinnamon

:::::

THE MUFFIN BATTER
Vegetable spray for the muffin pans (see Note)

1¾ cups all-purpose flour

1 tablespoon baking powder

1 teaspoon baking soda

¼ teaspoon salt

1 stick (½ cup) unsalted butter, at room temperature

½ cup sugar

2 large eggs

¼ teaspoon vanilla extract

1 cup buttermilk

¼ teaspoon ground cinnamon

⅛ teaspoon ground cardamom

---

1. Place a rack in the middle of the oven and preheat it to 375 degrees F.

2. *Make the swirl:* In a small bowl, mix together the walnuts, sugar, and cinnamon.

3. *Make the muffins:* Lightly coat 12 muffin cups with the vegetable spray.

4. In a small bowl, whisk together the flour, baking powder, baking soda, and salt and set aside. Beat the butter in a stand mixer with the paddle attachment or using a hand-held mixer on medium speed, until creamy. Add the sugar and beat for about 4 minutes, until light and fluffy. Add the eggs one at a time on low speed, using a spatula to scrape down the sides of the bowl. Add the vanilla and mix to combine.

5. Add half of the flour mixture and mix on low until blended. Add the buttermilk, cinnamon, and cardamom, and mix until smooth. Add the remaining flour mixture and mix until just blended.

6. Fill the prepared muffin cups halfway full. Sprinkle each with a tablespoon of the coffee cake swirl. Top with the remaining batter. Sprinkle a heaping teaspoon of the swirl on top of each muffin. Bake for about 22 minutes, or until the muffins are a pale golden brown and a toothpick

inserted in the center comes out clean. Cool the muffins in the pan for about 5 minutes and then, using a table knife,

gently lift the muffins out of their cups and place them on a cooling rack. Serve warm or at room temperature.

NOTE
Rather than greasing the pans, you can simply line them with a paper or foil liner.

Muffins, Scones & Coffee Cake

COCONUT-ORANGE-PECAN COFFEE CAKE

SERVES 12 | QUICK AND SIMPLE 🕐

This sour cream–based coffee cake has an unusually light, fresh-tasting filling and a topping made from unsweetened grated coconut, orange zest, and pecans. The cake will keep, tightly wrapped in plastic, at room temperature for several days, or it can be wrapped and frozen for several months.

Serve with fruit salad (page 30) and good, strong coffee.

INGREDIENTS

THE COCONUT-ORANGE-PECAN FILLING AND TOPPING

1¾ cups (6 ounces) coarsely chopped pecan halves

1½ cups unsweetened grated coconut

⅓ cup sugar

1½ tablespoons grated orange or tangerine zest

1 teaspoon ground cinnamon

½ stick (¼ cup) unsalted butter, cut into small cubes

THE CAKE BATTER

2 sticks (1 cup) unsalted butter, plus extra for the pan

2 cups all-purpose flour plus extra for the pan

1 teaspoon baking powder

½ teaspoon baking soda

Pinch of salt

1¼ cups sugar

2 large eggs

1 cup sour cream

2 tablespoons freshly squeezed orange or tangerine juice

1½ teaspoons grated orange or tangerine zest

1. *Make the filling/topping:* In a medium bowl, mix together the pecans, coconut, sugar, zest, and cinnamon. Add the butter and, using your hands or a pastry blender, work it into the mixture until it resembles coarse bread-crumbs. Set aside.

2. Place a rack in the middle of the oven and preheat it to 350 degrees F. Grease a 9½-inch tube pan with butter, flour it lightly, and tap it upside down to make sure no excess flour adheres. Set aside.

3. *Make the cake batter:* In a medium bowl, sift together the 2 cups flour, the baking powder, the baking soda, and salt, and set aside.

4. Beat the 2 sticks butter and the sugar in a stand mixer with the paddle attachment or using a hand-held mixer on medium speed for about 5 minutes, until it's light, fluffy, and pale. Use a spatula to scrape down the sides of the bowl and the paddle. Add the eggs one at a time, beating well after each addition. Reduce the mixer speed to low and add half of the flour mixture. Beat well until incorporated. Add half of the sour cream and all of the orange juice and zest, and beat well. Use a spatula to scrape down the sides of the bowl and paddle again if needed. Add the remaining flour and then the remaining sour cream and beat until the batter is smooth and fully incorporated.

5. The batter will be quite thick. Spoon half of it into the prepared pan. Sprinkle half of the filling/topping on top of the batter. Top with the remaining batter, using a spatula to smooth down the top. Sprinkle the remaining filling/topping on top and bake for 50 to 60 minutes, or until a toothpick inserted in the center comes out clean.

6. Remove the cake from the oven and let cool for about 20 minutes. Use a table knife to release the cake from the pan by running it around the edges of the pan and the tube in the middle. Invert the cake onto a serving plate and remove the pan. Re-invert the cake so the side with the coconut topping is facing up.

CHAPTER

FRUIT DISHES

BERRY SALAD WITH MINT SYRUP

SERVES 4 | QUICK AND SIMPLE ⏱

This fruit salad is bursting with freshness thanks to a simple herb-flavored syrup that infuses it. You can make it up to a few hours in advance, cover, and refrigerate until ready to serve. This recipe was adapted from one in our earlier book, *Stonewall Kitchen Favorites*.

INGREDIENTS

THE MINT SYRUP

½ cup sugar

¼ cup coarsely chopped fresh mint

: : : : :

THE BERRY SALAD

1 cup fresh raspberries

1 cup fresh blackberries

1 cup quartered fresh strawberries

½ cup fresh blueberries

Fresh mint leaves, for garnish

1. *Make the syrup:* Mix the sugar with 1 cup water in a saucepan and bring to a boil over high heat, stirring frequently to make sure the sugar is dissolved. Reduce the heat to low and add the mint; simmer for 10 more minutes. Strain the syrup into a small jar or bowl and cool. Leftover syrup will keep, covered and refrigerated, for 10 days and is great to use in iced tea and drinks like mojitos. Makes about ¾ cup.

2. *Make the salad:* In a medium bowl, gently mix together the berries. Taste the berries. If they are very sweet, you will need only 1 tablespoon mint syrup; add enough syrup—up to 2 tablespoons—to flavor the berries without oversweetening. Serve cold, garnished with mint leaves.

VARIATION
Tropical Fruit and Melon Salad with Lime Syrup
SERVES 4 TO 6

½ cup sugar

2 tablespoons fresh lime juice

1 teaspoon grated lime zest

1½ cups fresh honeydew melon balls (see Note)

1½ cups fresh cantaloupe melon balls (see Note)

1½ cups seedless fresh watermelon balls (see Note)

1 cup cubed fresh mango

1 cup cubed fresh pineapple

1 banana, cut into thin slices

Paper-thin slices of lime, for garnish

1. Make the syrup following the directions for the Mint Syrup, substituting the fresh lime juice and grated lime zest for the mint.

2. In a medium bowl, gently toss together the fruit. Add enough syrup to flavor the fruit without overwhelming it. Serve cold, garnished with the lime slices.

NOTE
To make melon balls, cut a small ripe melon in half and remove the seeds. Using a melon scooper or baller, scoop out balls from the melon flesh. If you don't have a scooper or baller, use a small spoon.

MEDITERRANEAN YOGURT BAR

Some of the best breakfasts we've ever had were in Mediterranean countries that make amazingly thick and silky yogurt. This is a great breakfast that's easy to put together for those mornings when you have guests, but no time to actually cook.

Put out a big bowl of Greek-style yogurt (or a locally made yogurt). If you can't find Greek yogurt, you can use plain yogurt (or vanilla-flavored yogurt) and place it in a fine-mesh strainer for about an hour. The liquid will drain out and you'll be left with a thick, creamy yogurt similar to Greek yogurt. Serve the yogurt with bowls of any or all of the following ingredients; each person sprinkles on their own ingredients to make an individual yogurt sundae.

* Walnuts, almonds, pistachios, and pine nuts (whole or coarsely chopped)

* Dried apricots, dates, and other dried fruit

* Honey or maple syrup

* Fresh fruit and berries

* Wedges or cubes of fresh melon

* Thin slivers of crystallized ginger

* Granola or bran cereal

* Thin slices of tomatoes and cucumbers dressed with olive oil, salt, and pepper

* Wedges of fresh or dried figs

* Crusty bread and country butter

BREAKFAST FRUIT SMOOTHIES

SERVES 1 TO 2 | QUICK AND SIMPLE 🕐

What we love most about smoothies for breakfast is that they only take about five minutes and contain everything you need for what nutritionists love to refer to as "a good, healthful, well-rounded breakfast."

We offer two variations on the smoothie here, but experiment with different fruits and combinations and find your own favorites. A note of explanation on why we use frozen fruit: There are now really good frozen organic fruits available year-round. They have all the flavor of good, ripe, fresh fruit and they add a natural thickener to the drink!

VANILLA-PEACH–BLOOD ORANGE SMOOTHIE

INGREDIENTS

1 cup frozen or fresh peach slices (see Note), reserve a couple of slices for garnish

½ cup vanilla-flavored low-fat yogurt

2 tablespoons freshly squeezed blood orange, navel orange, or clementine juice

¼ banana, sliced (optional)

Pinch of sugar (optional)

Place the peaches in the container of a blender and blend until smooth. Add the yogurt, orange juice, and banana (if using), and blend. Taste the mixture and see if it needs sugar (very ripe peaches will require no additional sugar). Serve in a tall glass with a straw, garnished with a peach slice or two.

NOTE

If using fresh fruit, you may need to add 1 to 2 crushed ice cubes to thicken the smoothie.

Continued . . .

...continued

WALKER'S BLACKBERRY-STRAWBERRY-BLUEBERRY-MAPLE SMOOTHIE

INGREDIENTS

½ cup organic frozen or fresh strawberries

½ cup organic frozen or fresh blueberries

½ cup plain low-fat yogurt

¼ cup organic frozen or fresh blackberries

¼ cup low-fat milk

1 tablespoon maple syrup

1 to 2 fresh mint leaves, for garnish (optional)

Place all the ingredients (except the mint leaves) in the container of a blender and blend until thick and smooth. Serve in a tall glass with a straw and a mint leaf (if desired).

VARIATIONS

Substitute any fresh or frozen fruit for the berries. Try cantaloupe, honeydew, watermelon, pears, nectarines, etc.

Substitute honey for the maple syrup.

Add 1 teaspoon or more of flax seed for extra omega-3s.

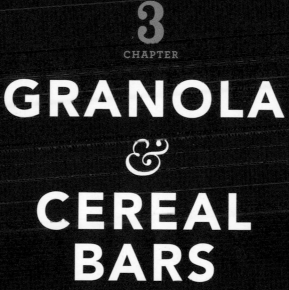

3

CHAPTER

GRANOLA
&
CEREAL
BARS

PERFECTLY GOOD GRANOLA

MAKES ABOUT 8 CUPS | QUICK AND SIMPLE 🕐

We've tasted all kinds of granola. Some are too sweet, while others are too chunky and overloaded with dried fruit and nuts. But this one, which we modestly title "Perfectly Good Granola," seems just right—good for you and bursting with fresh flavor and a chewy, crunchy texture. A mixture of oats, sunflower, and flax seeds, nuts, spices, and dried fruit, the granola is sweetened with maple syrup and blueberry honey (you can also use regular honey, but we just love the subtle flavor of blueberry in this).

This granola is the basis for the outrageously tasty Perfectly Good Granola Bars (page 40). Many of these ingredients are available in health food stores or in the health food section of your grocery store. You can substitute unsweetened coconut or dried blueberries or any type of nut or fruit for those listed here.

INGREDIENTS

Vegetable spray for the pans

3 cups rolled oats

1 cup (3 ounces) coarsely chopped pecans (see Note)

½ cup coarsely chopped dried apricots

½ cup raisins or currants

¼ cup roasted salted sunflower seeds

¼ cup flax seeds

¼ cup sesame seeds

¼ cup dried cranberries or cherries or blueberries

1½ teaspoons ground cinnamon

1 teaspoon ground ginger

½ cup canola oil

½ cup maple syrup

½ cup blueberry honey or any good-quality honey

1. Preheat the oven to 300 degrees F. Line two *rimmed* cookie sheets with parchment paper or aluminum foil and lightly coat with the vegetable spray.

2. In a large bowl, mix together the oats; pecans; apricots; raisins; sunflower, flax, and sesame seeds; cranberries; cinnamon; and ginger, and stir well to combine thoroughly. Add the oil,

maple syrup, and honey and mix well, making sure the liquids thoroughly coat the dry ingredients.

3. Divide the mixture between the two cookie sheets and press down with a metal spatula so the granola is about ½ inch thick. Bake for 40 to 45 minutes, or until the mixture is golden brown and looks cooked through, rotating the cookie sheets once during the baking. Let cool on the pans for 10 minutes and then separate the mixture into clumps (if you like a thick, clumpy type of granola) or separate the mixture thoroughly for a looser-style granola. The granola will keep in a well-sealed jar or plastic bag at room temperature for up to 1 week.

NOTE

For a nuttier flavor, lightly toast the nuts on a cookie sheet in a 350 degree F oven for about 10 minutes, or until lightly browned. Cool and chop before adding to the mixture.

VARIATIONS

Add ½ cup unsweetened grated coconut.

Add ½ cup pitted dates, coarsely chopped.

Add ⅓ cup pumpkin seeds.

Add walnut oil instead of the canola oil for a rich, nutty flavor.

Add 1 to 2 teaspoons grated orange zest.

PERFECTLY GOOD GRANOLA BARS

MAKES ABOUT 24 BARS | QUICK AND SIMPLE 🕐

This is the breakfast to grab when you're running late and don't even have time to boil water for coffee or tea. The bars are also delicious when you have lots of time, though, accompanied by a bowl of yogurt and fresh fruit.

INGREDIENTS
Vegetable spray for the pans
1 recipe of *uncooked* Perfectly Good Granola (page 38)

1. Place a rack in the middle of the oven and preheat the oven to 300 degrees F. Line one large rimmed cookie sheet or two smaller ones with parchment paper or aluminum foil and lightly coat with vegetable spray.

2. Place the uncooked granola mixture onto the sheet(s) and press down with a metal spatula to create a firm, even layer.

3. Bake on the middle shelf for 45 to 50 minutes, or until the granola is a pale golden brown. Remove from the oven and let cool for 10 minutes. Using a sharp knife, cut the granola into 25 bars and let cool thoroughly. The bars will keep in a tightly sealed tin at room temperature for up to 5 to 6 days.

WHY DOES THIS HOT CEREAL TASTE SO GOOD?

Any of these toppings will transform plain-old, hot cereal into something special:

* Drizzle on maple syrup, honey, brown sugar, or molasses.

* Add a teaspoon of Fruit Butter (page 128).

* **SPICE COMBO:** Mix ⅛ teaspoon each of ground cinnamon, ginger, allspice, and cardamom and keep in a well-sealed spice jar for several months. Sprinkle a dash on top of cereal to taste.

* **DRIED FRUIT:** Sprinkle on whole or coarsely chopped dried cranberries, cherries, raisins, currants, blueberries, apricots, or a combination of them all.

* **BERRIES:** Mix in ¼ cup fresh blueberries, sliced strawberries, and blackberries.

* **TOASTED NUTS:** Place 1 cup of your favorite nuts—walnuts, almonds, pistachios, pecans, hazelnuts—on a cookie sheet and bake at 350 degrees F for about 10 minutes, or until the kitchen starts to smell nutty. Let cool and coarsely chop. Sprinkle on as desired.

* **FLAX SEED AND BRAN:** To give your morning cereal a more "whole-grain life," sprinkle on 1 tablespoon of flax seed and/or bran flakes just before serving. The whole grains add not only great nutrients, but also a nice texture.

* Sprinkle on unsweetened coconut or sunflower or pumpkin seeds.

EGG
DISHES

NEW YORK–STYLE SMOKED SALMON SCRAMBLE

SERVES 2 TO 4 | QUICK AND SIMPLE 🕐

This New York–deli classic combines eggs scrambled with caramelized onions, smoked salmon, and cream cheese. Serve with toasted bagels or toast and cream cheese mixed with scallions (page 124). The recipe can easily be doubled or tripled to serve a crowd.

INGREDIENTS

2 teaspoons unsalted butter

1 medium-large onion, very thinly sliced

Salt

Freshly ground black pepper

4 large eggs

1 tablespoon chopped fresh dill, divided (optional)

4 slices smoked salmon (about 4 ounces), cut into 1-inch pieces

¼ cup cream cheese, cut into small cubes

1. In a medium skillet, heat the butter over low heat. When the butter is sizzling, add the onion and season with salt and pepper. Cook, stirring occasionally, for about 12 minutes, or until the onion is golden brown.

2. In a small bowl, whisk the eggs and season lightly with salt, pepper, and half of the dill (if using). Remember the salmon will be salty, so don't add too much salt.

3. Add the salmon to the hot skillet and cook for 1 minute, stirring it into the onion well. Raise the heat to medium-high and add the eggs. Add the cream cheese cubes on top of the eggs and let cook, untouched, for about 10 seconds. Using a fork or a soft spatula, scramble the eggs gently and cook for 2 to 3 minutes, or until the eggs are set. If you like your eggs firm you'll want to cook them about 3 minutes. Sprinkle the eggs with the remaining dill, if desired, and serve hot.

LONG AND SLOW OR HOT AND QUICK?

No, this is not the name of an X-rated movie. The three of us were sitting around one morning talking about scrambled eggs (this sort of thing happens when you're immersed in the subject of breakfast). "Do you scramble your eggs long and slow over very low heat?" someone asked. "Yes," answered two of us. "No!" said the other. "I like them fast over high heat." So the testing began.

Turns out that long and slow wins out: Crack 2 or 3 or even 8 eggs in a bowl and whisk them up with a fork with salt and pepper and a touch of dairy if you like (1 tablespoon of milk or cream per 2 eggs). Heat a medium skillet over very low heat with 1 teaspoon butter per egg (you could also use olive oil but it's a different sort of experience) and then cook the eggs very slowly—a good 4 to 5 minutes, scrambling them with the fork every now and then. The result is scrambled eggs that are lighter, fluffier, and—dare we say—more elegant than eggs cooked in a hot skillet and scrambled quickly in just a minute or two.

This is the basic recipe, but there are endless variations. Add minced chives or chopped fresh herbs; grated cheese; crumbled or finely chopped ham, bacon, or pancetta; roasted or raw red, green, or yellow bell peppers; mushrooms; chopped zucchini; or virtually any vegetable or left-over you have on hand.

HUEVOS RANCHEROS

SERVES 4

We are huge fans of this classic, hearty Mexican egg dish. We first created this recipe for our book, *Stonewall Kitchen Favorites*, and tried to come up with an even better version for this book. But truth be told, these huevos are just right.

INGREDIENTS

3 tablespoons olive oil

1 small red onion, chopped

1 small yellow onion, chopped

Salt

Freshly ground black pepper

Two 15-ounce cans black beans, drained and rinsed

½ teaspoon ground cumin

2 tablespoons chopped fresh cilantro leaves

Hot pepper sauce

Four 6-inch corn tortillas

4 large eggs

1½ cups shredded Monterey Jack cheese

About ½ cup sour cream

About 1 cup guacamole, store-bought or homemade

2 cups salsa, store-bought or homemade

1. Preheat the oven to 300 degrees F.

2. Heat 1 tablespoon of the oil in a large skillet over medium heat. Add the red and yellow onions and season with salt and pepper. Cook, stirring, until the onions are soft, about 5 minutes. Add the beans and cumin, and cook over low heat for 5 minutes more, stirring occasionally. Stir in 1 tablespoon of the cilantro and a dash or two of hot sauce; season again with salt and pepper, and set aside. (The beans can be made a day ahead; cover and refrigerate. Place over low heat to rewarm. If they seem dry, add 1 to 2 tablespoons water.)

3. Wrap the tortillas in a clean, damp kitchen towel. Place in the oven and heat for 5 minutes.

4. Meanwhile, heat 1 tablespoon of the remaining oil in a large skillet over medium heat. Crack 2 eggs (or more if they fit without overlapping) into the pan and fry for 1 to 2 minutes on each side, or until the egg whites solidify, depending on how soft you like your eggs. Transfer to a warm plate and repeat with the remaining oil and eggs.

5. Place 1 warm tortilla on each of 4 plates. Divide the beans among the 4 tortillas. Sprinkle the cheese over the beans, and top each plate with a fried egg. Garnish with sour cream, guacamole, and the remaining cilantro. Surround the tortillas with a small dollop of the salsa. Serve hot sauce on the side.

EGGS BAKED IN PANCETTA CUPS

SERVES 6

This is one of those dishes that can only be as good as the ingredients you work with. Look for really good farm-fresh eggs. Then look for good pancetta, a cured (not smoked) Italian bacon with a salty and peppery flavor, which is available in most supermarkets. However, if you have an Italian grocery store or a really good meat market nearby, look for pancetta that can be sliced to order. Ideally you'll work with Italian-made pancetta that is sliced about ⅛ inch thick. Two good ingredients. One amazing recipe that can be done from start to finish in about 25 minutes.

You can serve the pancetta and eggs straight from the oven accompanied by crusty bread or place them on top of mixed salad greens. You could also add a few tablespoons of chopped fresh herbs or cubed tomatoes to the egg for a variation.

INGREDIENTS

About 6 slices pancetta (about 7 ounces), sliced about ⅛ inch thick (see Note)

6 large fresh eggs

Salt

Freshly ground black pepper

1. Place a rack in the middle of the oven and preheat the oven to 400 degrees F.

2. Press each pancetta slice into a muffin cup, molding it into the cup so that it covers the entire bottom and sides.

Bake the pancetta for 8 minutes, or until it begins to crisp. Remove from the oven and crack an egg directly into each pancetta cup. Sprinkle each one very lightly with salt and pepper. Bake for another 8 to 10 minutes, or until the egg white is set and the yolk looks almost cooked. When you gently jiggle the muffin pan, the yolks should wobble somewhat but not look raw.

3. Remove from the oven and let cool for about 1 minute. Gently run a table knife around the sides and bottom of the pancetta (being careful not to pierce the eggs). Use a thin metal or off-set spatula to remove the eggs and pancetta in 1 piece.

4. Serve hot, accompanied by toast, crusty bread, or a tossed salad.

NOTE

If you are working with presliced supermarket-brand pancetta, you may need 12 slices, overlapping them slightly to fill each muffin cup.

PROVENÇAL-STYLE BAKED EGGS

SERVES 4

We love the simplicity and fresh flavors of this baked egg dish: sautéd tomatoes with scallions and fresh herbs layered in a ramekin (a small, ovenproof bowl) with a raw egg and grated cheese. Serve with an assortment of toast, jellies, cheeses, honey, and fruit.

INGREDIENTS

1 tablespoon olive oil

3 scallions, chopped

1 tablespoon finely chopped fresh thyme or 1 teaspoon dried or use half basil and half thyme

1 large tomato, finely chopped

Salt

Freshly ground black pepper

8 teaspoons grated Parmesan cheese or your favorite hard cheese

4 large eggs

4 teaspoons heavy cream

1. Place a rack in the middle of the oven and preheat the oven to 400 degrees F.

2. In a medium skillet, heat the oil over medium-low heat. Add the scallions and thyme and cook for 1 minute. Add the tomato, season with salt and pepper, and stir for 1 minute, until the tomato is softened. Remove from the heat.

3. In the bottom of four ¾-cup ramekins (or 6-ounce oven-proof custard cups, 4 inches across), spread 1½ tablespoons of the tomato mixture, and sprinkle on 1 teaspoon grated cheese. Crack 1 egg on top of the tomato/cheese in each ramekin and add another tea-spoon of cheese; season with salt and pepper. Add ½ table-spoon of the tomato mixture on top of each and drizzle with 1 teaspoon cream.

4. Bake for about 12 minutes, or until the whites are set but the yolks still look runny. You can very gently jiggle the ramekins to make sure the eggs are not too raw; the cook-ing time will depend on the freshness of your eggs and the type of ramekin. Remove from the oven and serve hot in the ramekins.

VARIATIONS

Add sautéed artichoke hearts, zucchini, or peppers.

Substitute different herbs and cheeses.

PORTUGUESE-STYLE POACHED EGGS WITH LINGUIÇA AND SWISS CHARD

SERVES 4

Linguiça, a Portuguese-style sausage that bursts with flavor, pairs well with Swiss chard, kale, or even spinach. The sautéed mixture is served with a poached egg on top and a splash of hot pepper sauce. Thick slices of crusty bread or toast would also be delicious.

INGREDIENTS

1 pound linguiça sausage, cut into ½-inch pieces

1 cup boiling water

1½ pounds Swiss chard, kale, spinach, or your favorite greens, well cleaned, dried, and coarsely chopped

4 scallions, cut into 1-inch pieces

Salt

Freshly ground black pepper

4 large eggs

Hot pepper sauce

1. Bring a large pot of water to a simmer for the eggs.

2. Put the sausage in a large skillet and add the 1 cup boiling water. Cook over medium-high heat until the water has evaporated, about 10 minutes. Be sure to flip the sausage pieces over once or twice so they cook evenly on both sides.

3. When the water has evaporated, add the chard in handfuls, stirring well to incorporate all the greens into the skillet. There should be enough oil from the sausages but if the pan appears dry, add about ½ cup of water.

4. Add the scallions, season with salt and pepper, and stir, cooking for about 10 minutes,

until the greens are tender. Taste for seasoning.

5. Crack the eggs into the simmering water one at a time. Use a spoon to swirl the water around the eggs, to keep them in motion and prevent the egg whites from spreading out too much. Let the eggs simmer for 2½ to 3 minutes, or until the whites are set and the yolks are just beginning to set (see Perfect Poaching, page 54). Remove the eggs from the water with a slotted spoon and be sure to drain them.

6. Divide the sausage and greens among 4 plates. Place a poached egg on top of each and add a small splash of hot pepper sauce on top of the eggs. Serve hot.

PERFECT POACHING

What is it about poaching eggs that fills cooks with such fear? The technique is simple and easy: Bring a pot or a skillet full of water to a gentle simmer. You don't want a rapid boil or the eggs will cook too quickly. Crack an egg into a small bowl and gently slide it into the middle of the simmering water. Use a spoon to swirl the water around the egg, to keep it in motion and prevent the egg white from spreading out too much. Let the egg simmer for 2½ to 3 minutes, depending on how firm you like your egg (very runny yolk or not so much) and how fresh your eggs are (very fresh eggs will cook faster). Typically, a perfect poached egg has a runny yolk and a firm white. Remove the egg with a slotted spoon, making sure to drain any excess water off it before serving. You can make a picture-perfect egg by using a small knife or biscuit cutter to trim the edges into an evenly round shape.

If you're poaching eggs for a crowd (for a Benedict-style dish, for instance), you can pre-poach the eggs and finish them off at the last minute. Poach the eggs for 2 minutes or until the whites are just set. Carefully lift them out and place on paper towels. Keep the pot of water and just before serving, heat to a gentle simmer. Carefully place the poached eggs into the hot water and cook for an additional minute, until hot and cooked through. Serve hot.

OMELET WITH TOMATOES, CHEESE, AND FINES HERBES

SERVES 1 | QUICK AND SIMPLE 🕐

This is the basic recipe for that beloved French classic, the omelet. Consider this a master plan and let your innovations and experiments begin. You can add any sort of meat, vegetable, cheese, spices, or herbs (see Variations). For a two-egg omelet (which will serve one), you'll want a generous half a cup of filling. If you're serving omelets for a party, we suggest making the fillings ahead of time (simply double or triple as needed) and preparing the omelets one at a time just before serving.

INGREDIENTS

2½ teaspoons olive oil or butter

⅓ cup diced fresh tomatoes

1 tablespoon minced fresh chives

1 tablespoon finely chopped fresh basil

1 teaspoon finely chopped fresh tarragon

Salt

Freshly ground black pepper

2 large eggs

1 tablespoon milk

¼ cup grated or crumbled cheese, such as Cheddar, Parmesan, Gruyère, goat, or feta

1. Heat 1 teaspoon of the oil in a heavy 8-inch skillet over low heat. Add the tomatoes; half of the chives, basil, and tarragon; and season with salt and pepper. Cook for 1 to 2 minutes, or until the tomatoes just begin to soften. Remove the mixture to a plate.

2. In a small bowl, whisk together the eggs; milk; remaining chives, basil, and tarragon; and season with salt and pepper.

3. Heat the remaining 1½ teaspoons of the oil in the same skillet set over medium-low heat. Add the eggs and let set for 30 seconds. Add the tomato mixture and cheese to half of the omelet and let cook for about 1 minute. Using a spatula (metal or silicone), lift 1 corner of the omelet up and tilt the pan to let the raw egg in the middle of the pan drip underneath. Continue to do this for another minute until there is very little raw

Continued...

...continued

egg apparent. Using the spatula, gently flip the half of the omelet that has no filling over the half of the omelet with the filling. Let cook for another minute, until the eggs look cooked and the cheese is melted. If you like your omelet very dry, cook for another minute. Carefully slide the omelet onto a serving plate.

VARIATIONS

There are endless variations for omelets. The basic technique for fillings is to precook vegetables until almost done, and precook meat (bacon, sausage, etc.) thoroughly. Here are a few of our favorite combinations:

* Sausage, greens, and Cheddar

* Zucchini, tomato, and mozzarella

* Smoked trout, dill, and cream cheese

* Lobster, chives, and crème fraîche

* Potato, bacon, and onion

* Brie, smoked ham, and mushrooms

* Caramelized onion, feta, and olives

* Three kinds of mushrooms and Gruyère

* Spinach, onion, and mozzarella

* Spring asparagus, feta, and chives

* Red, green, and yellow bell peppers with goat cheese

* Tapenade, tomato, and basil

SPINACH, FETA, AND TOMATO FRITTATA

SERVES 4

There are few foods more adaptable and forgiving than a frittata. For those who have a fear of making omelets, a frittata is simple, easy, and produces dramatic results. In this version, you sauté fresh spinach and cherry tomatoes and mix the eggs with crumbled feta cheese, but the possibilities are endless. The frittata is baked in the oven and finished off under the broiler to produce a slightly puffed dish that's like a cross between a soufflé and a crustless quiche.

We've found that a smaller, ovenproof skillet is your best bet. An 8½-inch skillet is ideal for a six-egg frittata. You don't want to use a skillet any larger or the frittata will be too thin, won't puff up, and can dry out. The smaller skillet produces creamy eggs with a good, thick height.

INGREDIENTS

2 tablespoons olive oil

1 cup packed stemmed raw spinach or baby spinach with stems

Salt

Freshly ground black pepper

¾ cup cherry tomatoes, quartered if large and halved if small, or ¾ cup cubed fresh tomatoes

1 tablespoon chopped fresh thyme or basil or 1 teaspoon dried

6 large eggs

2 tablespoons grated Parmesan cheese

¼ cup crumbled feta cheese

1. Place a rack in the middle of the oven and preheat the oven to 425 degrees F.

2. In a heavy, ovenproof 8½-inch skillet, heat 1 tablespoon of the oil over medium-high heat. Add the spinach in batches, seasoning with salt and pepper, and stirring well. Cook until wilted and soft, 2 to 3 minutes. Remove the spinach to a plate.

3. Add the remaining 1 tablespoon of oil to the skillet over medium heat. Add the tomatoes, half of the thyme, season with salt and pepper, and cook for 2 minutes over low heat.

4. Meanwhile, in a medium bowl, whisk together the eggs, the remaining thyme, and the Parmesan until frothy. Season with salt and pepper.

5. Add the spinach back into the skillet and stir together with the tomatoes. Add the egg mixture and sprinkle the feta on top in an even layer. Let cook for 1 minute just to set the eggs.

6. Bake for 15 minutes, or until the frittata is beginning to puff up and the eggs look set. Then place under the broiler for about 2 minutes, or until the eggs are puffed slightly and look cooked. Remove and serve in wedges hot, at room temperature, or cold.

VARIATIONS

Add crumbled bacon, ham, sausage, or pancetta.

Substitute different cheeses and vegetables as you like, such as:

* Asparagus, red pepper, and goat cheese

* Zucchini, Parmesan, and fennel

* Red, green, and yellow bell pepper strips with grated Gruyère and fresh basil

Egg Dishes

CRUSTLESS BREAKFAST QUICHE

SERVES 6 | QUICK AND SIMPLE 🕐

Quiche is ideal breakfast food—eggs, bacon, cheese, and vegetables. But who has time to deal with the crust? Here we eliminate it, make a quick batter, and bake it directly in a muffin pan. The quiche bakes for a mere 25 minutes, making this a very doable breakfast for any day of the week. You can also save time by making the batter the night before and baking just before serving.

INGREDIENTS

Vegetable spray for the muffin pans

4 slices pancetta (5 ounces), sliced about ⅛ inch thick; or 4 slices thick country-style bacon; or ½ cup cubed cooked ham

½ cup sour cream

½ cup crème fraîche

2 large eggs

1 teaspoon chopped fresh thyme

Salt

Freshly ground black pepper

½ cup grated Parmesan cheese

1. Place a rack in the middle of the oven and preheat the oven to 350 degrees F. Lightly coat six muffin cups with the vegetable spray and set aside.

2. In a medium skillet, cook the pancetta or bacon until crisp on each side, 3 to 5 minutes per side for the pancetta and 4 to 6 minutes per side for the bacon; drain on paper towels and cut into small pieces.

3. In a large bowl, lightly beat together the sour cream, crème fraîche, and eggs. Add half of the thyme, then season with salt and pepper. Stir in the Parmesan.

4. Fill the prepared muffin cups two-thirds full. Bake for 25 minutes, rotating the pan once during the cooking time, until golden brown and solid when you jiggle the pan. Let the quiches cool for 5 minutes before removing from the cups. Sprinkle with the remaining thyme and serve immediately.

VARIATIONS

For a vegetarian version, sauté ½ cup sliced peppers, onions, mushrooms, or any vegetables until just cooked and add instead of the meat.

Add grated sharp Cheddar, crumbled goat or feta, or your favorite cheese instead of, or in addition to, the Parmesan.

GREENS, SAUSAGE, AND CHEDDAR BREAKFAST STRATA

SERVES 8

Picture a savory bread pudding layered with sautéed onions, greens, sausage (both hot and sweet), and sharp Cheddar cheese in a thyme-scented custard and you'll get an idea of how good this breakfast strata really is. There are a few steps to making this savory dish, but it actually couldn't be simpler. Best of all, the strata needs to sit for at least 1 hour and up to 8 hours, so the whole thing can be prepared ahead of time, and simply popped into the oven about an hour before your guests arrive. This is a whole meal in one pan, ideal for a brunch or special breakfast gathering. Serve with fruit salad (page 30), coffee, and tea.

The sausage can easily be omitted to make this a vegetarian dish; simply double the amount of greens and onions. The strata can be served hot or at room temperature.

INGREDIENTS

1½ tablespoons olive oil

1 medium onion, thinly sliced

Salt

Freshly ground black pepper

8 ounces greens (baby spinach, spinach, kale, chard, etc.), stemmed and chopped if the leaves are large

1 pound pork sausage (8 ounces sweet and 8 ounces hot)

1 tablespoon unsalted butter

9 cups 1-inch bread cubes (about 1 large loaf or 2 baguettes; see Note)

2 cups grated sharp Cheddar cheese

8 large eggs

2 cups milk

1½ tablespoons chopped fresh thyme or 1½ teaspoons dried

1. In a large skillet, heat 1 tablespoon of the oil over low heat. Add the onion and season well with salt and pepper; cook for 10 minutes, stirring occasionally, until the onion is pale golden. Add the greens in batches, stirring them into the onion and cooking for about 5 minutes, or until they are just wilted. Remove to a plate.

Continued…

…continued

Let sit for 5 minutes and then place another plate of the same size on top and squeeze out the liquid from the greens. Set aside.

2. Add the remaining ½ tablespoon of oil to the same skillet over medium heat. Squeeze the sausage meat out of the casings (discarding the casings) and, using a spatula, crumble the meat into small pieces. Cook for 10 minutes, stirring frequently, until cooked through. Drain on paper towels and set aside.

3. Grease a 3-quart gratin dish (14 by 10 or 13 by 9 inches) with the butter. Line the bottom of the pan with half of the bread, creating an even layer. Scatter half of the greens and onion mixture on top of the bread. Scatter half of the sausage on top. Finally, add half of the cheese on top. Repeat with the remaining bread, greens/onion, sausage, and cheese.

4. In a large bowl, whisk together the eggs and milk. Add a generous dash of salt and pepper and the thyme and whisk vigorously. Pour the mixture evenly over the bread. Cover with plastic wrap and refrigerate for 1 hour and up to 8 hours.

5. Place a rack in the middle of the oven and preheat the oven to 350 degrees F. Bring the strata to room temperature before baking. Bake the strata for 45 to 50 minutes, or until the egg custard is completely set and the top of the strata is golden brown. Let sit for 5 to 10 minutes before serving.

NOTE
Like good stuffing, a good strata depends on good bread. Use bits and pieces of leftover bread (be sure it's not moldy or rock hard) and feel free to use a variety. We've made strata using leftover crusty French and Italian bread, olive breads, rye, white, wheat, etc. And be sure to use the bread crust for a good texture.

LOBSTER BENEDICT WITH
MEYER LEMON–SCALLION BUTTER

SERVES 2

You want something special that will make an impression? Look no further. This egg dish—which combines poached eggs with cooked lobster meat lightly drizzled with a lemony butter—is simple to put together and totally satisfying. If you buy precooked lobster meat (try to buy tail meat as it is the part everyone really wants), the dish can be put together in about 15 minutes! This meal is very rich and one egg and half a muffin should be more than enough for each person; you can always double or triple the recipe for a party.

If you can't find Meyer lemons, which are available during the winter months, you can substitute regular lemons.

INGREDIENTS

**THE MEYER LEMON–
SCALLION BUTTER**

½ stick (¼ cup) unsalted butter

1 scallion, finely chopped

1 tablespoon freshly squeezed
Meyer lemon juice or regular
lemon juice

1 teaspoon grated Meyer lemon
zest or regular lemon zest

1½ teaspoons minced fresh
chives

: : : : :

2 large eggs

1 English muffin, 2 thick slices
bread, or 2 biscuits

3½ ounces cooked lobster meat
(about 2 tails), cut into long,
thick strips

1 scallion, cut into long, very
thin strips

2 paper-thin slices Meyer or
regular lemon

1. *Make the butter:* In a small saucepan, melt the butter over low heat. Add the scallion, lemon juice and zest, and the chives, and let cook for about 2 minutes, or until bubbling. Set aside and keep warm.

2. Bring a medium pot of water to a simmer. Crack the eggs into the water one at a time. Use a spoon to swirl the
Continued…

Egg Dishes

...continued
water around the eggs, to keep them in motion and prevent the egg whites from spreading out too much. Let the eggs simmer for 2½ to 3 minutes, or until the whites are set and the yolks are just beginning to set (see Perfect Poaching, page 54). Remove the eggs from the water with a slotted spoon and be sure to drain them.

3. While the eggs are poaching, toast the English muffin or bread, or heat the biscuits in a low oven. Place the lobster meat in the hot lemon butter and let it warm up over low heat for 1 to 2 minutes.

4. Place half of the toasted English muffin on a plate. Top with a poached egg. Remove half of the lobster from the butter with a slotted spoon (draining well) and place on the egg. Spoon about 2 tablespoons of the lemon butter on top, and garnish with a scallion strip and a slice of the lemon. Repeat with the remaining ingredients.

SMOKED SALMON AND ARUGULA BENEDICT WITH ARUGULA-LEMON BUTTER

SERVES 2 TO 4

In this recipe we do away with the heaviness of traditional Eggs Benedict and offer a lighter, fresher take on the classic. Out goes the meat, replaced with smoked salmon and bright, tangy arugula leaves placed on an English muffin (or your favorite bread), topped with a perfectly poached egg and a light Arugula-Lemon Butter.

INGREDIENTS

THE ARUGULA-LEMON BUTTER

1 cup packed stemmed raw arugula leaves

½ stick (¼ cup) butter

1 tablespoon freshly squeezed lemon juice

1 teaspoon grated lemon zest

Pinch of sea salt

Pinch of freshly ground black pepper

: : : : :

4 large eggs

2 regular or whole-wheat English muffins or four 1-inch-thick slices of your favorite bread

8 thin slices smoked salmon

½ cup packed stemmed raw arugula leaves

1. *Make the butter:* Pulse the arugula in a food processor until it is coarsely chopped.

2. Melt the butter in a small saucepan. Add the arugula, lemon juice and zest, and the salt and the pepper and cook for 2 minutes, or until the arugula is just wilted. Set aside or keep warm over very low heat.

3. Bring a medium pot of water to a simmer. Crack the eggs into the water one at a time. Use a spoon to swirl the water around the eggs, to keep them in motion and prevent the egg whites from spreading out too much. Let the eggs simmer for 2½ to 3 minutes, or until the whites are set and the yolks are just beginning to set (see Perfect Poaching, page 54). Remove the eggs from the water with a slotted spoon and be sure to drain them.

4. Toast the muffins until golden brown. Place a muffin half (or 2) on each plate and top each with 2 slices of salmon, making sure they overlap the muffin slightly so you'll see the color once the egg goes on top. Divide the arugula leaves among the muffins on top of the salmon.

5. Warm the Arugula-Lemon Butter over low heat if necessary. Drain the eggs well and place 1 on each muffin. Spoon 1 to 2 tablespoons of the warm butter on top and serve hot.

VARIATIONS

Use smoked trout or your favorite smoked fish (cut into small chunks or thinly sliced) instead of the smoked salmon.

Substitute Breakfast Crab Cakes (page 70) for the smoked salmon.

Substitute baby spinach for the arugula for a milder version.

BREAKFAST CRAB CAKES

MAKES ABOUT TEN 2-INCH CAKES; SERVES 4 TO 5

Fish cakes (made from cod, haddock, and other white fish) have long been a traditional breakfast favorite throughout northern New England. In this recipe, fresh Maine crabmeat is mixed with sweet red pepper, onion, and scallion and then coated in panko breadcrumbs for a good crunchy exterior. Serve the crab cakes with a lemon wedge, fried eggs, and toast. They are also excellent topped with a poached egg (see page 54) and drizzled with Meyer Lemon–Scallion Butter (page 65) or Arugula-Lemon Butter (page 68). Make a pot of coffee, pull out the Sunday paper, and enjoy.

INGREDIENTS

3½ tablespoons olive oil

1 medium onion, minced, about ¾ cup

1 small red bell pepper, finely chopped, about ½ cup

1 scallion, white and green parts, finely chopped

Salt

Freshly ground black pepper

8 ounces fresh Maine lump crabmeat

⅓ cup finely chopped fresh parsley

6 large eggs, 1 lightly beaten

About 1 cup panko breadcrumbs (coarse Japanese-style breadcrumbs)

1. In a medium skillet, heat 1½ tablespoons of the oil over very low heat. Add the onion and cook for 8 minutes, stirring well, until it turns a pale golden color. Add the bell pepper and scallion, season with salt and pepper, and cook for another 4 minutes, until the bell pepper has softened. Remove from the heat and let cool.

2. In a medium bowl, gently mix together the crabmeat, parsley, and the beaten egg until well incorporated. Add the cooled onion/bell pepper mixture and about ¼ cup of the panko or enough so that when you form a cake, the mixture holds together; you may need to add another 1 to 2 tablespoons of panko depending on the size of your egg.

3. Place the remaining breadcrumbs in a shallow bowl. Use a ¼-cup measure to help form the cakes. Lightly coat each side of the crab cakes in the breadcrumbs, pressing lightly to make sure they adhere. (There should be a very light breadcrumb coating.)

4. In a large skillet, heat the remaining 2 tablespoons of the oil over medium heat. Add

several crab cakes to the hot skillet at a time, being sure not to crowd the skillet. Cook for about 3 minutes on each side, or until golden brown and cooked through. Drain the cakes on paper towels. Repeat with the remaining cakes.

5. Cook the remaining 5 eggs as desired and divide among individual serving plates. Serve with one or two crab cakes.

CHAPTER

BREAKFAST SANDWICHES, SALAD

&

PIZZA

SPANISH TOMATO TOAST WITH CHEESE AND BASIL (*PAN CON TOMATE*)

SERVES 2 TO 4 | QUICK AND SIMPLE 🕐

In little bars and cafés throughout Spain, morning begins with a cup of strong coffee and *pan con tomate*—grilled bread lightly brushed with olive oil and topped with grated fresh tomato. It may sound odd eating tomato toast for breakfast, but give it a try and you'll soon see why this is such a popular morning treat. You can keep it simple, but we love this best topped with crumbled cheese—goat, feta, or grated Parmesan—and a fresh basil leaf.

INGREDIENTS

2 medium-sized ripe tomatoes

Salt

Freshly ground black pepper

2 large fresh basil leaves, cut into thin strips

Four 1-inch-thick slices ciabatta or good crusty bread

2 tablespoons fruity olive oil

¼ cup grated or crumbled cheese, such as a good Spanish manchego, or Parmesan, goat cheese, or feta

1. Preheat the broiler.

2. Using the large openings of a box grater, grate the tomatoes into a small bowl. Season with salt and pepper and add half of the basil.

3. Place the bread on a cookie sheet and, using a pastry brush or the back of a spoon, brush on half of the oil. Place under the broiler for about 1 minute, or until just golden brown. Flip the bread over and sprinkle on the cheese; broil for another 30 seconds to 1 minute, until golden brown and the cheese is bubbling. Alternatively you can simply broil the other side of the bread and sprinkle the cheese on top of the tomato at the end.

4. Spoon the grated tomato on top of the cheese toast and drizzle with the remaining olive oil and basil. Add a light seasoning of salt and pepper.

OPEN-FACED BREAKFAST SANDWICH WITH PEQUILLO PEPPERS

SERVES 2 | QUICK AND SIMPLE 🕐

Blue Ribbon Bakery, located on Downing Street in lower Manhattan, is the kind of bakery you dream about. Gorgeous whole-grain breads are stacked next to ciabatta and olive breads, baguettes, and an amazing collection of Mexican honeys. One day, we spotted open-faced egg sandwiches topped with sweet pequillo peppers. This is our version of that delicious breakfast sandwich.

Thick whole-grain bread is toasted and spread with a saffron- and rosemary-flecked mayonnaise (if the idea of mayonnaise is not to your liking, particularly in the morning, you can use butter as the base), then topped with thin slices of hard-boiled eggs and strips of pequillo peppers. Pequillos are sweet, red, Spanish pickled peppers that can be found in gourmet food stores. If you can't find them, you can always substitute roasted red bell pepper strips mixed with a teaspoon of white wine vinegar.

INGREDIENTS

2 thick slices whole-grain bread or crusty French bread

2 tablespoons mayonnaise or butter

1 teaspoon finely chopped fresh rosemary or ½ teaspoon finely chopped dried

⅛ teaspoon Spanish saffron, crumbled (or a pinch of sweet paprika)

Salt

Freshly ground black pepper

2 eggs, hard boiled (see page 80) and thinly sliced

2 tablespoons thinly sliced pequillo or sweet piquante peppers

1. Toast the bread until golden.

2. In a small bowl, mix together the mayonnaise with the rosemary and saffron. Season with salt and pepper.

3. Spread each piece of toast with 1 tablespoon of the saffron-rosemary mixture. Divide the eggs between each piece of toast, overlapping the

slices. Arrange the peppers on top of the eggs and sprinkle liberally with salt and pepper.

VARIATION

Fry the eggs in a touch of olive oil instead of hard boiling them. Place the fried eggs, yolk-side up, on top of the toast.

B.E.L.T. (BACON, EGG, LETTUCE, AND TOMATO) SANDWICH WITH TARRAGON-LEMON MAYONNAISE

SERVES 2 | QUICK AND SIMPLE 🕐

If a BLT is the perfect sandwich combination, than a B.E.L.T is even better. The meaty crunch of bacon combined with a juicy tomato; slices of hard-boiled egg; crunchy, refreshing lettuce; and a simple tarragon-and-lemon-infused mayonnaise on golden brown toast is, in our opinion, perfect breakfast fare. The idea for this unusual breakfast sandwich came from The Market Basket, a gourmet food take-out shop in Rockport, Maine. The eggs, bacon, and tarragon-flavored mayonnaise can all be made ahead of time, making the sandwich easy to put together in minutes just before serving.

Use any leftover tarragon mayonnaise for other sandwiches or as the base of a creamy vinaigrette.

INGREDIENTS	
2 large eggs	Salt
4 slices of thick country-style bacon	Freshly ground black pepper
2 tablespoons mayonnaise	4 slices white bread
2 teaspoons chopped fresh tarragon	1 medium-sized ripe tomato (about 2½ ounces), cut into 4 thick slices
2 teaspoons chopped fresh chives	4 romaine lettuce leaves
1 teaspoon freshly squeezed lemon juice	

1. Place the eggs in a medium pot and cover with cold water. Hard boil the eggs (see Hard Boiled: Hot and Cold, page 80). Peel them and cut into ⅛-inch slices.

2. Place the bacon in a medium skillet set over medium-low heat and cook for 4 to 6 minutes on each

Continued...

...*continued*

side, depending on the thickness, until cooked through. Drain on paper towels.

3. In a small bowl, gently mix the mayonnaise, tarragon, chives, and lemon juice and season with salt and pepper. (The eggs, bacon, and mayonnaise can be made a day ahead of time. Cover and refrigerate until ready to assemble the sandwiches.)

4. When you're ready to eat, toast the bread and while it's toasting, gather all the ingredients into a line for assembly.

5. Spread each piece of warm toast with 1 tablespoon of the tarragon mayonnaise. Place 2 tomato slices, 4 egg slices, 2 bacon pieces, and 2 lettuce leaves on 2 slices of the toast. Top each with a remaining slice of toast and cut the sandwiches into halves.

HARD BOILED: HOT AND COLD

HELPFUL HINTS

Hard boiling an egg is a simple act, but there are a few little "tricks" that can mean the difference between under- or overcooked eggs, and eggs that are easy to peel versus ones that won't seem to peel no matter what you do.

Place the eggs in a saucepan large enough to hold them without having them touch or bump up to one another. Cover completely with cold water and bring to a gentle boil over high heat. As soon as the water boils, reduce the heat to low, cover the pot, and cook over a very gentle simmer for 8 minutes. Remove from the heat and let sit for 1 minute. Carefully drain the hot water and fill the pot with cold water while it's in the sink, letting it run over until the pot is filled with cold water. Let it sit for a minute. Pour off the cold water and gently swirl the pot so that the eggs gently crack against the sides. Fill the pot with cold water again and let it sit for another minute. The cold water will pull the shells away from the (cooked) eggs and make it (very) easy to peel them.

BREAKFAST SALAD WITH BACON, FRIED EGGS, AND CROÛTES

SERVES 4

Salad for breakfast? Sure, why not? This breakfast dish—ideal for brunch and weekend entertaining—is refreshing, light, and totally satisfying. It combines a breakfast salad with fried eggs, bacon, and toast. It's an innovative twist on a French bistro salad.

INGREDIENTS

THE VINAIGRETTE
1 teaspoon Dijon-style mustard

Salt

Freshly ground black pepper

2 tablespoons red or white wine vinegar

2 tablespoons freshly squeezed lemon juice

½ cup olive oil

: : : : :

8 slices thick country-style bacon (about 8 ounces)

Eight 1-inch slices French bread or any crusty bread

3½ tablespoons olive oil

1 pound romaine or crunchy lettuce

4 large eggs

1. *Make the vinaigrette:* In a small bowl, stir together the mustard and salt and pepper to taste. Add the vinegar and lemon juice. Whisk in the oil and taste for seasoning. The vinaigrette can be made a day ahead of time; cover and refrigerate until ready to assemble the salad.

2. In a large skillet, cook the bacon over medium-low heat for 4 to 6 minutes per side, or until golden brown and crisp. Drain on paper towels. The bacon can be made several hours ahead of time and kept at room temperature.

3. Preheat the broiler. Place the bread slices on a cookie sheet. Using the back of a spoon or a pastry brush, lightly brush the bread with 1 tablespoon of the oil. Broil for 1 to 2 minutes, or until golden brown and just beginning to toast.

4. Remove from the oven and flip the bread over. Brush with another tablespoon of oil and broil for another 1 to 2 minutes, or until the bread is crisp and golden brown, being careful not to let it burn. The croûtes can be made several hours ahead of time, or overnight. Keep in a tightly sealed plastic bag.

5. Place the lettuce in a large salad bowl or in a large, deep platter. Just before serving, *Continued…*

…continued

add half of the vinaigrette and toss well.

6. Heat a large skillet over medium heat. Add the remaining 1½ tablespoons oil and let heat for a minute. Crack in the eggs, one at a time (if the skillet isn't big enough to fry all 4 eggs at the same time, divide the oil between 2 medium-sized skillets), and fry for about 2 minutes, or until the edges begin to turn brown and the whites are set. Gently flip the eggs over and cook for another minute. Gently place the eggs on top of the salad. Set the bacon slices on top of the eggs (or along the sides) and place the croûtes along the edges of the bowl or platter. Serve immediately, with the remaining vinaigrette on the side.

VARIATION

Rather than plain croûtes, make Parmesan croûtes: Place bread slices on a cookie sheet. Using a pastry brush or the back of a spoon, brush the toasts with the oil and sprinkle each with 1 tablespoon grated Parmesan cheese and broil until the cheese melts, 1 to 2 minutes. Flip the toasts over and brush with the oil and sprinkle with more Parmesan and broil until melted.

BREAKFAST PIZZA

EACH PIZZA SERVES 2 TO 4

You like to think of yourself as a person with an open mind. You believe you're always ready to experience new things. So open up to the possibility of a pizza for breakfast—topped with fresh mozzarella cheese, slices of ripe tomato, fresh basil strips, bacon, and eggs baked right on top of the whole thing. If you use premade pizza dough, the whole dish takes under 30 minutes from start to finish. The idea is to bake the pizza until the egg white is set and the yolk is still somewhat runny so that when you slice it into wedges, the yolk breaks open and spills on the cheese, tomato, bacon, and crust.

INGREDIENTS

6 slices thick country-style bacon (8 ounces)

Flour, for dusting

1 pound uncooked pizza dough, from the refrigerated section of your grocery store, a pizza parlor, or homemade

3 tablespoons olive oil

2 medium-sized ripe tomatoes, thinly sliced

1 pound fresh mozzarella, thinly sliced

¼ cup thinly sliced fresh basil leaves

4 large eggs

Salt

Freshly ground black pepper

1. Place a rack in the middle of the oven and preheat the oven to 425 degrees F.

2. Cook the bacon in a large skillet until it is *almost* crisp, 3 to 5 minutes on each side, depending on the thickness. Drain on paper towels. Cut each piece of bacon in half crosswise and set aside.

3. Lightly flour a work surface. Cut the dough in half. Roll out half of the dough into an oblong or round shape about 10 inches by 7 inches. Place on a clean cookie sheet. Spread 1 tablespoon of the oil on the dough and, using a pastry brush or your fingers, rub it gently over the dough, making sure it covers the whole surface.

4. Arrange half of the tomato slices on the dough. Place half of the cheese slices on top and in between the tomatoes. Sprinkle with ½ tablespoon of the oil and bake for 5 minutes. Remove from the oven and scatter half of the basil over the tomatoes. Arrange half of the bacon on top and very carefully crack 2 eggs into the center of the pizza. (If you feel confident, crack them directly on the pizza; if not crack them into a small bowl, one at a time, and carefully arrange them in the middle of

the pizza.) Sprinkle the eggs and the whole pizza with salt and pepper.

5. Bake for another 10 to 12 minutes, or until the egg whites look set (gently wobble the pan to see if the egg whites look solid); the yolks should still be a little wobbly, and the crust should look cooked and golden brown. Remove from the oven; let sit for 1 minute before cutting into slices or wedges. Repeat with the remaining pizza ingredients. The yolk should spill out when the pizza is sliced.

VARIATION
Use pancetta instead of bacon. Cook for 2 to 4 minutes on each side.

CHAPTER

PANCAKES, FRENCH TOAST
& WAFFLES

BREAKFAST CORN FRITTERS

MAKES ABOUT 10 SMALL FRITTERS; SERVES 3 TO 4

If the idea of eating corn for breakfast strikes you as strange, you haven't tried these fritters. They're packed full of sweet, fresh corn; eggs; and milk, formed into small pancakes (or fritters), and drizzled with maple syrup.

INGREDIENTS

½ cup all-purpose flour

½ teaspoon baking powder

Pinch of salt

¼ cup milk

1 to 2 tablespoons sugar (optional; see Note)

1 large egg, lightly beaten

2 cups fresh corn kernels, cut off 2 large cobs (or 2 cups frozen corn, if you must)

Vegetable or olive oil for the pan

Maple syrup, for serving

About 1 tablespoon butter for garnish, optional

1. In a large bowl, sift together the flour, baking powder, and salt. Add the milk and sugar (if using), and whisk until smooth. Beat in the egg and gently mix in the corn.

2. In a large skillet, heat about 3 tablespoons oil over medium-high heat. Drop 2 to 3 tablespoons batter into the hot oil and carefully flatten the mixture with the back of a spatula to form a fritter. Cook for 2 to 3 minutes on each side, or until golden brown. Repeat with the remaining batter.

3. Serve hot accompanied by maple syrup with a dollop of butter placed on top of the hot fritters, if desired.

NOTE

If your corn is very fresh and sweet you won't need to add any sugar, but if the corn is frozen or not just-picked, you may want to sweeten it with the addition of some sugar.

SILVER DOLLAR POTATO PANCAKES

MAKES ABOUT TWELVE 2-INCH PANCAKES; SERVES 5 TO 6

This recipe is a cross between bite-sized pancakes and perfect home fries. The key to making them is to let the grated potatoes sit for about 10 minutes and then, using your hands, wring the liquidy starch out of them. Serve these golden brown cakes with sour cream, crème fraîche, or thick Greek-style yogurt or applesauce. They are delicious accompanied by a fried egg or omelet (page 55).

INGREDIENTS

2 large potatoes
(about 1 pound), peeled
(Yukon Gold are perfect)

1 large egg

1½ tablespoons fresh
minced chives

About 2½ tablespoons
all-purpose flour

Salt

Freshly ground black pepper

2 to 3 tablespoons vegetable oil

Accompaniments:
about 1 cup sour cream,
crème fraîche, or Greek-style
yogurt; and/or applesauce

1. Grate the potatoes on the coarse side of a large box grater into a large bowl. Let sit for 10 to 15 minutes. Using your hands, squeeze the grated potatoes to release the brown starchy liquid; discard the liquid.

2. In a medium bowl, whisk the egg and add the potatoes. Add 1½ tablespoons fresh minced chives. Add 2 tablespoons of the flour and a generous dash of salt and pepper. If the mixture seems to hold together, it's fine; if not, add the additional ½ tablespoon flour.

3. Heat a large skillet over medium heat. Add 1 tablespoon of the oil and let it get hot for about 1 minute (see How Hot is Hot?, page 96).

Carefully place a heaping tablespoon of the mixture—about 2 inches wide and 1 inch thick—into the hot skillet for each pancake. Let cook, undisturbed, for 3 minutes. Gently flip the pancakes over and, using your spatula, gently flatten them just slightly. Cook for another 4 to 5 minutes, adding more oil if needed, or until the pancakes are a rich golden brown on each side and cooked through and tender. (Cut one open to test.)

4. Drain on paper towels and serve hot with accompaniments. (You can also make them ahead of time and reheat them on a cookie sheet in a 300 degree F oven for about 10 minutes, but they're never quite as good.)

GOOD-FOR-YOU WHOLE-GRAIN BLUEBERRY PANCAKES

MAKES ABOUT 16 THREE-INCH PANCAKES; SERVES 4 TO 5 | QUICK AND SIMPLE 🕐

Making pancakes with whole-grain flour that are light, fluffy, and appealing (as opposed to heavy and laden) is not as easy as it sounds. After much experimenting we love this version, which combines whole-wheat flour and white flour with buttermilk and fresh blueberries. For an extra whole-grain twist, you can sprinkle on some bran flakes with the blueberries if you like. If you make the pancake batter ahead of time, you can cook the pancakes in just minutes.

Serve with maple syrup or make a quick maple-blueberry syrup by simmering 1 cup maple syrup and 1 cup blueberries (fresh or frozen) over low heat for 5 to 8 minutes, or until the blueberries soften.

INGREDIENTS

1 cup whole-wheat flour

1 cup unbleached white flour

2 teaspoons baking powder

¼ teaspoon baking soda

¼ teaspoon salt

2 cups buttermilk

2 large eggs, lightly whisked

2½ tablespoons unsalted butter, melted, plus extra for greasing the griddle

2 tablespoons maple syrup

About 1½ cups fresh or frozen blueberries, raspberries, blackberries, or strawberries, sliced

¼ to ⅓ cup bran (optional)

1. In a large bowl, whisk together the whole-wheat flour, white flour, baking powder, baking soda, and salt. Whisk in the buttermilk, eggs, melted butter, and syrup and mix until just blended.

2. Heat a large griddle or skillet over medium heat. Add only enough butter to lightly grease the griddle. Working in batches, add about ¼ cup batter to the hot skillet for each pancake, making pancakes about 3 inches wide. Scatter as many blueberries as you like on top of each pancake (and sprinkle lightly with bran, if desired), and let cook for 2½ to 3 minutes on each side, or until lightly golden brown and cooked through.

3. Serve hot or keep warm in a 300 degree F oven. Serve topped with maple syrup or blueberry-maple syrup (see head note).

WALNUT PANCAKES WITH MAPLE-GLAZED APPLES

MAKES 8 TO 9 PANCAKES

Fluffy, nutty, and perfumed with allspice, these pancakes are topped with apple slices lightly cooked in maple syrup. Serve with extra warm syrup on the side. This recipe makes about 8 pancakes, but can easily be doubled to serve a crowd.

INGREDIENTS

THE PANCAKE BATTER

1 cup all-purpose flour

1 cup (4 ounces) finely chopped toasted walnuts (see Note)

¾ teaspoon baking powder

¼ teaspoon salt

1 large egg

1 cup buttermilk

2 tablespoons unsalted butter, melted

1 tablespoon maple syrup

THE MAPLE-GLAZED APPLES

1 tablespoon unsalted butter

2 apples, such as Macoun, Jonathan, Delicious, or your favorite variety, peeled (optional), cored, and cut into ½-inch-thick slices

⅛ teaspoon ground allspice

Pinch of ground nutmeg

3 tablespoons maple syrup, plus 1 cup for serving (optional)

Canola oil

1. *Make the pancake batter:* In a small bowl, whisk together the flour, walnuts, baking powder, and salt and set aside. In a large bowl, whisk the egg. Whisk in the buttermilk, butter, and maple syrup. Add the flour mixture to the wet ingredients and blend until just incorporated, using a light touch. Set aside and let sit for 15 minutes and up to several hours. (If making several hours ahead, cover and refrigerate until ready to cook the pancakes. Bring the batter to room temperature before using.)

2. *Meanwhile, prepare the apples:* Melt the butter in a medium skillet set over medium heat. Add the apple slices, sprinkle with the allspice and nutmeg, and cook for 1 minute, gently stirring. Add the 3 tablespoons maple syrup and cook for 2 minutes, gently stirring, until the apples look glazed or caramelized. Remove from the heat and set aside.

3. Preheat the oven to 300 degrees F. Heat a large skillet or griddle over medium heat. Brush it lightly with the oil. When the pan is hot (see How Hot is Hot?, page 96), add ¼ cup pancake batter to the pan. Add another 2 or 3 pancakes, depending on *Continued...*

...*continued*

the size of the skillet and making sure not to overcrowd the pan. Place 3 or 4 of the apple slices on top of each pancake, gently pressing them into the batter. Cook for 2 minutes, or until bubbles begin to surface and the pancakes appear golden brown on the underside. Gently flip the pancakes and cook for another 2 to 3 minutes, or until the apples are caramelized and the pancakes are golden brown. Serve immediately or place on an ovenproof plate and keep warm in the preheated oven. Repeat with the remaining batter and apples. Heat any remaining apples in the skillet until warm and serve on the side or spoon on top of the pancakes. Place 1 cup of maple syrup in a small saucepan and warm over low heat. Serve the warm syrup on the side, if desired.

NOTE

Lightly toast the nuts on a cookie sheet in a 350 degree F oven for about 10 minutes, or until lightly browned. Remove from the oven and pulse in a food processor or blender.

You don't want the nuts to be like sawdust; they should be just finely ground. If you buy finely chopped walnuts, toast them in a 350 degree F oven for 10 minutes, or until very lightly toasted.

VARIATIONS

Substitute pears for the apples.

Substitute almonds or pecans for the walnuts.

Add a dash of ground cardamom to the pancake batter.

HOW HOT IS HOT?

HELPFUL HINTS

It's always a little tricky figuring out when pancake griddles, waffle irons, and crêpe pans are hot enough and ready to cook. Here's a little trick: Heat the pan with just a very light brushing of oil or butter and place over medium or medium-high heat. After about 2 minutes, place your hand over the pan. If it feels comfortably warm (meaning you can keep your hand there without any fear of burning it), it's not ready. You want the pan to be hot enough so you can feel the heat, but don't really want to keep your hand there too long. Add the batter and if it seems to be cooking too rapidly—bubbles forming very quickly and immediate browning on the underside of the pancake—it's too hot. Reduce the heat (or take the skillet off the heat) and proceed. The trick: You want it hot enough to cook efficiently, but not so hot that you burn the pancakes.

BASIC FRENCH CRÊPES

MAKES 20 CRÊPES

If you've always thought of crêpes as fussy French food, think again. The batter takes 5 minutes to whip up in a blender and the crêpes cook in minutes. You can make the basic batter and use the crêpes for blintzes (page 100), add chopped fresh herbs and grated lemon zest for savory pancakes, or top the plain crêpes with everything from jam to fruits to chocolate (see Variations).

There are a few basic steps to keep in mind when making crêpes. The batter needs to sit, refrigerated, for at least 1 hour. And you'll need a good (meaning heavy) 8-inch skillet with a 7-inch base. And, don't be discouraged if your first crêpe is less than perfect—they often are.

INGREDIENTS

1½ cups low-fat milk

3 large eggs

1½ cups all-purpose flour

5 tablespoons unsalted butter, melted

½ teaspoon salt

About ⅓ cup canola oil

1. In a blender, mix the milk and eggs until well blended. Add the flour, butter, and salt and blend until frothy and thoroughly mixed. Cover and refrigerate for at least 1 hour and up to 6 hours.

2. Heat a heavy 8-inch skillet over medium heat. Using a pastry brush, lightly oil the bottom of the pan. The skillet is hot enough when you place your hand several inches above it and it feels very hot (see How Hot is Hot?, page 96). Add about 3 tablespoons batter (the easiest way is to pour it from a small ladle) to the skillet, swirling it around so that you have the thinnest possible covering on the bottom of the pan. The crêpe should be very thin and coat the entire bottom of the skillet. Let cook for about 1 minute, or until the crêpe starts to set. Use a small metal or off-set spatula, and carefully lift the crêpe up from the base of the skillet and flip it over. Cook for another minute or so on the other side. The crêpe should be a pale golden brown. Set aside on a large plate.

3. Repeat with the remaining batter. You can stack the crêpes gently on top of each *Continued…*

…continued

other and reheat later, depending on how you're serving them. If making them ahead of time, stack them with a small piece of waxed paper between each crêpe to keep them from sticking together.

VARIATIONS
Sweet Crêpes
Add ¼ cup sugar to the batter and cook the crêpes according to the directions. Serve hot, spread with any of the following fillings:

Jam: Brush your favorite type of jelly or jam on the hot crêpe and roll up in a cigar shape.

Chocolate: Brush with about 1 tablespoon of a chocolate spread like Nutella or finely grate about 1 tablespoon of your favorite type of chocolate bar and sprinkle on a hot crêpe. Roll into a cigar shape.

Maple: Serve the hot crêpes with warm or room-temperature maple syrup.

Fruit: Fill the hot crêpes with berries, pieces of cut citrus, or your favorite fruit.

Lemon Curd: Fill the hot crêpes with about 1 tablespoon lemon curd and roll up in a cigar shape.

Savory Crêpes
Add freshly ground black pepper, 1 tablespoon chopped fresh herbs, and 1 teaspoon grated lemon zest to the batter and cook according to the directions. Serve hot, spread with any of the following fillings:

Lemon-Herb: Add 1 tablespoon finely chopped fresh rosemary, chives, and thyme to the batter. Serve with melted butter flavored with fresh lemon juice and more chopped herbs.

Arugula-Lemon Butter (page 68): Serve the warm crêpes drizzled with the butter.

Cheese and Ham: Fill a hot crêpe with about 2 tablespoons grated cheese and 1½ tablespoons chopped cooked ham. Fold in half.

Asparagus and Goat Cheese: Roll a hot crêpe around 2 or 3 cooked asparagus spears and 2 tablespoons crumbled goat cheese.

Chicken: Fill a hot crêpe with 2 tablespoons cooked chicken (cut into thin strips), 1 tablespoon roasted red bell pepper, and 2 tablespoons diced grilled portobello mushrooms.

BLINTZES TWO WAYS: SWEET AND SAVORY

MAKES 6 BLINTZES; SERVES 3

An old Jewish favorite, blintzes are thin French-style crêpes rolled around a sweet filling (ricotta and cottage cheese mixed with cinnamon, vanilla, and sugar) or a savory one (ricotta and cottage cheese mixed with salt, pepper, fresh chives, and lemon zest), lightly drizzled with butter and baked. The sweet blintzes are served here with maple syrup. If you've only had fried blintzes, you'll be pleased to see how light and satisfying baked blintzes can be. Choose the sweet or savory filling (or double the number of crêpes you make and try both of them). The crêpes and the fillings can be made ahead of time and assembled just before baking.

INGREDIENTS

SWEET FILLING

½ cup large-curd cottage cheese

½ cup whole-milk ricotta cheese

1½ tablespoons sugar

1 tablespoon unsalted butter, melted

½ teaspoon ground cinnamon

¼ teaspoon vanilla extract

: : : : :

SAVORY FILLING

½ cup large-curd cottage cheese

½ cup whole-milk ricotta cheese

1 tablespoon unsalted butter, melted

2 tablespoons minced fresh chives

1 teaspoon grated lemon zest

Salt

Freshly ground black pepper

: : : : :

6 Basic French Crêpes (page 97)

1 tablespoon unsalted butter, melted

1. *For the sweet filling:* In a medium bowl, mix together the cottage and ricotta cheeses. Add the sugar, butter, cinnamon, and vanilla and mix well.

2. *For the savory filling:* In a medium bowl, mix together the cottage and ricotta cheeses. Add the butter, chives, zest, and a generous amount of salt and pepper. (The fillings can be covered and refrigerated for several hours before assembling the blintzes.)

3. Place a crêpe on a clean work surface. Spread a heaping tablespoon of filling just below the center of the crêpe. Fold the bottom of the crêpe upward to enclose the filling. Fold both sides toward the inside to enfold the filling completely. Roll up the crêpe into a packet and place in a rimmed baking dish or a shallow gratin dish with the seam side down. Repeat with the remaining crêpes and filling. (The blintzes can be covered and refrigerated for several hours before baking.)

4. Preheat the oven to 350 degrees F. Drizzle the 1 tablespoon melted butter on top of the blintzes and bake for 15 to 20 minutes, or until hot. Let them sit for 5 minutes before serving to let the filling set. Sprinkle the remaining chives over the savory blintzes, if desired.

SPICED BRIOCHE FRENCH TOAST WITH MAPLE PEARS AND APPLES

SERVES 2 TO 4

When you cook thick-sliced French toast, do it slowly so that the heat has time to travel all the way to the center of each piece of bread and cook it through before the edges burn. If you're cooking for a crowd, pile the finished toasts onto a baking sheet in a warm oven as you finish cooking them. Keep them loosely covered with foil, so they don't dry out before you top them with sweet, buttery sautéed pears and apples.

This recipe comes from food writer Jess Thomson, who writes a wonderful blog called Hogwash (http://jessthomson.wordpress.com).

INGREDIENTS	
THE FRENCH TOAST	**THE PEAR AND APPLE**
½ cup milk	1 tablespoon unsalted butter
3 large eggs	¼ teaspoon ground cinnamon
½ teaspoon vanilla extract	¼ teaspoon ground cardamom or allspice
¼ teaspoon ground cinnamon	1 Gala apple, thinly sliced
¼ teaspoon ground cardamom or allspice	1 Bosc pear, peeled and thinly sliced (optional)
⅛ teaspoon salt	2 tablespoons high-quality maple syrup, plus more for serving
Four 1-inch-thick slices day-old brioche loaf or white, wheat, or French bread	
Vegetable spray for the skillet or griddle	

1. *Make the French Toast:* Whisk the milk, eggs, vanilla, cinnamon, cardamom, and salt together in a pie plate or shallow bowl. Working with one piece at a time, dip the bread into the egg mixture, letting it sit for a minute or two on each side so the liquid soaks all the way through to the center of the bread.

2. Heat a large nonstick skillet or griddle over medium heat (see How Hot is Hot?, page 96). *Continued…*

…continued

When hot, lightly coat the pan with the vegetable spray and cook the bread (in multiple batches, if necessary) for 3 to 4 minutes per side, or until nicely browned and firm in the center.

3. *Make the Pear and Apple:* While the bread cooks, melt the butter in a nonstick skillet over medium-high heat. When melted, add the cinnamon and cardamom, stir to blend, and then add the apple and pear slices. Cook, stirring occasionally, until the fruit begins to brown, about 3 minutes. Add the 2 tablespoons maple syrup, simmer for 1 minute, and set aside.

4. Pile the pears and apples on top of the brioche toast, and serve warm, topped with additional syrup, if desired.

CHOCOLATE WAFFLES WITH CHOCOLATE-MAPLE SAUCE

MAKES ABOUT 8 SMALL WAFFLES

Even though this book is devoted to the morning meal, we had to have at least one recipe with chocolate. This decadent dish is for the kid in us all—something to splurge on for a weekend breakfast. Don't worry too much; there's only a tablespoon of sugar in the batter and low-fat buttermilk gives the waffles a rich flavor.

Top the waffles with a chocolate and maple syrup sauce, fresh berries, and a dollop of sour cream or crème fraîche. You could always garnish the dish with some shaved or finely chopped chocolate!

If you don't have a waffle iron, you can use the batter to make chocolate pancakes.

INGREDIENTS

THE CHOCOLATE-MAPLE SAUCE

2 ounces dark chocolate (64% cacao)

½ cup maple syrup

:::::

THE WAFFLE BATTER

3 tablespoons unsalted butter

2 ounces dark chocolate (64% cacao)

1 cup all-purpose flour

1 tablespoon sugar

1 teaspoon baking powder

½ teaspoon baking soda

¼ teaspoon salt

1 cup buttermilk

1 large egg

Vegetable oil for greasing the waffle iron

:::::

1 cup mixed fresh berries (blueberries, raspberries, and thinly sliced strawberries)

½ cup sour cream or crème fraîche

1. *Make the sauce:* In a small saucepan, melt the chocolate over very low heat. Add the maple syrup and stir to mix. Keep on very low heat.

2. *Make the waffle batter:* In a small saucepan set over very low heat, melt the butter and chocolate together until smooth. Remove from the heat.

3. In a large bowl, whisk together the flour, sugar,

Continued...

…continued
baking powder, baking soda, and salt.

4. In a separate bowl, whisk together the buttermilk, egg, and the butter/chocolate mixture until smooth. Slowly whisk in the flour mixture and incorporate just until the batter is smooth. (You can make the batter several hours ahead of time.)

5. Heat a waffle iron until hot (see How Hot is Hot?, page 96). Lightly grease the iron with the vegetable oil by using a pastry brush or a lightly oiled paper towel. Add ⅓ cup batter to the hot waffle iron, close the lid, and cook for about 1 minute, or until golden and crispy. Remove the waffle from the iron and serve hot with the Chocolate-Maple Sauce and the berries and sour cream.

CHAPTER 7

SIDE
DISHES

PAN-FRIED BREAKFAST TOMATOES AND ZUCCHINI

SERVES 2 TO 4 | QUICK AND SIMPLE 🕐

Every summer when the garden seems to be taken over by ripe tomatoes and zucchini, we try to think of new ways to use the overflow of vegetables. Turns out that quickly sautéed tomato and zucchini slices, lightly coated in seasoned panko breadcrumbs, makes a great breakfast. Serve the vegetables with fried eggs, omelets (page 55), frittata (page 58) or simply with crusty bread (perfect for sopping up the tomato juices) and a good fruit salad (page 30). The recipe can easily be doubled or tripled.

INGREDIENTS

1 cup plain or seasoned panko breadcrumbs (coarse Japanese-style breadcrumbs)

¼ cup all-purpose flour

2 tablespoons very thinly sliced fresh basil

Salt

Freshly ground black pepper

1 medium-sized ripe tomato, cut into ½-inch-thick slices

1 medium zucchini (about 8 ounces), cut into ½-inch-thick slices

1 tablespoon olive or canola oil

1 teaspoon unsalted butter

1. Preheat the oven to 300 degrees F.

2. Place the panko, flour, half of the basil, and a generous dash of salt and pepper on a large plate and mix well.

3. Lightly coat the tomato and zucchini slices in the seasoned breadcrumb mixture, pressing the vegetables gently into the mixture to make sure it adheres well.

4. Heat a large, heavy skillet (cast iron is ideal) over medium heat. Add the oil and butter and heat for 10 to 20 seconds, or until almost sizzling. Working in small batches, being careful not to overcrowd the skillet, add the zucchini and cook for about 3 minutes on each side, or until golden brown and tender. Place the cooked zucchini on an ovenproof plate and keep warm in the preheated oven.

5. Then cook the tomatoes for 2 to 3 minutes per side, until crisp on the outside and soft (but not falling apart) on the inside. The time will depend greatly on the ripeness and freshness of the tomatoes and zucchini and the type of skillet you use.

6. Serve immediately with a sprinkling of the remaining basil on top; the vegetables tend to "wilt" if they sit around too long.

ROASTED SWEET POTATO HOME FRIES

SERVES 4 TO 6 | QUICK AND SIMPLE 🕐

We love home fries with just about every type of breakfast dish, but they can be greasy and heavy. Here we roast sweet potatoes and sweet onions with just a touch of olive oil and plenty of fresh herbs.

You can make the home fries ahead of time (in which case you should undercook them just slightly), then crisp and heat them up in a skillet (with about a teaspoon of olive oil) over medium-high heat just before serving.

INGREDIENTS

2 large sweet potatoes (about 2 pounds), peeled and cut into 1-inch cubes

1 medium sweet-variety onion, such as Vidalia, chopped into ½-inch pieces

2 tablespoons olive oil

1 tablespoon chopped fresh thyme

1 tablespoon chopped fresh rosemary

Salt

Freshly ground black pepper

1. Place a rack in the middle of the oven and preheat the oven to 425 degrees F.

2. Place the potatoes, onion, oil, herbs, and salt and pepper to taste on a large cookie sheet, baking tray, or oven-proof skillet and toss well to coat all the ingredients with the oil.

3. Bake for 25 minutes, tossing the mixture once during the roasting time. (Remove from the oven at this point if making them ahead of time.) Raise the oven temperature to 475 degrees F and bake for another 5 to 10 minutes, or until the potatoes are tender and crisping up with golden brown edges.

VARIATIONS

Stir 1 cup finely chopped ham, bacon, or sausage (removed from the casing) into the mixture.

Stir in ¾ cup chopped sweet red, green, or yellow bell peppers.

Substitute creamy white potatoes (such as Yukon Gold) for the sweet potatoes, increasing the roasting time by 5 minutes.

Add a dash of cayenne or hot pepper sauce toward the end of the roasting time.

BLOOD ORANGE–GLAZED SAUSAGES

SERVES 2 TO 4 | QUICK AND SIMPLE 🕐

Go ahead and pour your orange juice on top of your sausages! The result: sweet, gooey, deliciously glazed sausages with no extra fat. Simply cook your favorite ones (we like sweet fresh pork sausages) in a skillet with water. When the water has evaporated, add some freshly squeezed orange juice and cook until the sausage is glazed with a gorgeous orange hue. If you can find fresh blood oranges (look during the winter months when they're in season), they add a beautiful blood orange color.

INGREDIENTS

2 fresh pork or other sausages (about 6 ounces), sweet or hot

⅔ cup freshly squeezed blood orange or regular orange juice

1. Place the sausages in a medium skillet, pour 1¾ cups water on top, and place over high heat. Cook, turning the sausages several times for about 10 minutes, or until the water has almost completely evaporated. When there's only 1 to 2 tablespoons of water left in the skillet, reduce the heat to medium and watch it carefully so it doesn't burn.

2. When the water has evaporated, add the orange juice and cook, turning the sausages from side to side so that they get evenly coated, until the orange juice becomes thick and syrupy, about 5 minutes. Remove from the heat and serve hot.

NOTE
You can cook the sausages in the water ahead of time and finish them off with the orange juice just before serving. Be sure to get the skillet really hot before adding the orange juice if the pan has cooled down.

TURKEY AND SAGE SAUSAGE PATTIES

MAKES 12 PATTIES; SERVES 4 TO 6

We wanted to see if it was possible to make a sausage patty without a lot of fat, but one that was full of good flavor. So we began experimenting. Turns out that when you combine ground turkey (an exceptionally lean, flavorful meat) with just a touch of ground pork (very fatty and full of flavor) and add in some fresh herbs, grated onion, and spices, you get a great breakfast sausage. We also tried the recipe using half turkey and half pork for a fuller flavor, and it's delicious (though clearly fattier).

These sausage patties taste best eaten hot right out of the pan, but they will hold for several hours; reheat them in a 250 degree F oven until warmed through, about 8 minutes.

INGREDIENTS

12 ounces ground turkey (96% lean)

4 ounces ground pork

2 tablespoons grated onion (grate on the large holes of a box grater)

1 tablespoon chopped fresh sage or 1 teaspoon dried and crumbled

2 teaspoons minced fresh garlic

2 teaspoons chopped fresh thyme or 1 teaspoon dried and crumbled

⅛ teaspoon chili powder

Salt

Freshly ground black pepper

About 1 tablespoon canola or vegetable oil

1. In a large bowl, thoroughly mix together the turkey, pork, onion, sage, garlic, thyme, chili powder, and a generous amount of salt and pepper.

2. Lightly wet your hands and shape the mixture into 12 round patties, about 2 inches across by ½ inch thick. (The patties can be made and formed several hours ahead of time; cover and refrigerate until ready to cook.)

3. Heat a large skillet over medium heat. Add half of the oil (you only need a touch), and cook the sausages in batches (adding the remaining oil as needed), making sure not to crowd the skillet. Cook for 4 minutes. Gently flip them over and cook for another 4 minutes, until they're cooked through. To test, cut one in half to make sure there is no sign of pinkness. Serve hot or set aside and reheat just before serving.

MAPLE-GLAZED HAM SLICES

SERVES 2 | QUICK AND SIMPLE 🕐

This is a great way to use any leftover ham from a holiday meal, or transform deli ham into a breakfast treat. The recipe only requires three ingredients— ham, butter, and maple syrup—so they all have to be top quality. You heat a skillet with just a touch of butter, add thick slices of cooked ham, and then glaze with maple syrup. The syrup and the butter caramelize into a sweet, gooey glaze and make an almost candy-like coating on the meat. Serve with fried or scrambled eggs, an omelet (page 55), frittata (page 58), pancakes or waffles (page 90, page 93, page 95, and page 105), and thick slices of toast. The recipe can be easily doubled or tripled for a crowd.

INGREDIENTS

2 teaspoons unsalted butter

2 slices cooked ham, about ¼ inch thick

¼ cup maple syrup

1. Heat a medium skillet over medium heat. Add the butter and cook until melted and sizzling. Add the ham and cook for 1 minute. Add half of the syrup and cook for 2 minutes. Carefully flip the meat over and add the remaining syrup.

2. Raise the heat to medium-high and cook for another 2 to 4 minutes, or until the syrup has thickened and coats the ham. Flip the ham once more to make sure both sides are evenly coated with the maple glaze.

3. Serve the ham and spoon any glaze remaining in the skillet on top.

GLAZED BACON THREE WAYS: MAPLE-GLAZED; CHILE POWDER AND BROWN SUGAR–GLAZED; AND FRENCH HERB AND BROWN SUGAR–GLAZED

QUICK AND SIMPLE 🕐

There are few foods more satisfying than bacon—the meaty flavor, the perfect ratio of fat to meat, and that thoroughly enticing come-to-the-table-now aroma. But we wondered if bacon could possibly taste even better if we added a few spices, herbs, and sweeteners to create a quick glaze? The answer is a resounding yes! Here we've created three quick, simple glazes for bacon. Use the best bacon you can find (we prefer a thick-sliced country-style bacon, but you can use virtually any type) and experiment with your own flavor combinations.

MAPLE-GLAZED BACON

SERVES 4

Maple syrup and bacon are good friends. The sweet syrup is the perfect counterpoint to the salty meat. Here we simply broil thick country-style bacon (which means all the fat drips into the bottom of the pan and is separated from the meat) and brush on good maple syrup to create the glaze.

INGREDIENTS

⅓ cup maple syrup

8 slices bacon, preferably thick country-style

1. Preheat the broiler. Place the syrup in a small bowl and have a small pastry brush ready. Lay the bacon on the rack of a broiler pan and place under the broiler for 1 minute, with the oven door slightly ajar. Brush each piece generously with maple syrup and place under the broiler for another 1 to 2 minutes, or until the bacon looks cooked and glazed with the syrup.

Turn the broiler pan once while it's cooking to ensure even browning. Watch the bacon carefully to make sure it doesn't burn.

2. Very carefully, using tongs, flip the bacon over and broil for 1 to 2 minutes more. Brush generously with maple syrup and broil for another minute, turning the pan halfway through the cooking time. The bacon is ready when it's cooked and has a thick maple glaze. Let cool for 30 seconds before serving; it will be very hot.

Continued ...

...*continued*

CHILE POWDER AND BROWN SUGAR– GLAZED BACON

SERVES 3

A mild red chile powder and brown sugar create a perfect balance of heat and sweet. You can use a mild New Mexican ground chile or choose something a bit spicier.

INGREDIENTS
⅓ cup packed light brown sugar
1½ teaspoons mild ground red chile powder
Freshly ground black pepper
6 strips bacon, preferably thick country-style

1. Mix the brown sugar, chile powder, and a generous amount of pepper in a medium shallow bowl and combine thoroughly. Coat the bacon strips, one at a time, by dipping the raw bacon into the bowl of spices and coating well on both sides. You may need to use your hands to press the mixture onto the bacon so it adheres well.

2. Preheat the broiler. Lay the bacon on the rack of a broiler pan and place under the broiler for 1 to 3 minutes, with the oven door slightly ajar, or until the bacon looks cooked and is bubbling and glazed. Turn the broiler pan once while it's cooking to ensure even browning. Watch the bacon carefully to make sure it doesn't burn.

3. Very carefully, using tongs, flip the bacon over and broil for 1 to 2 minutes more, turning the pan halfway through the cooking time. The bacon is ready when it's cooked and the glaze is bubbling. Let cool for 30 seconds before serving; it will be very hot.

FRENCH HERB AND BROWN SUGAR– GLAZED BACON

SERVES 3

You can use any combination of fresh or dried herbs in this recipe.

INGREDIENTS
⅓ cup packed light brown sugar
1 tablespoon finely chopped fresh rosemary or 1 teaspoon dried and crumbled
1 tablespoon finely chopped fresh thyme or 1 teaspoon dried and crumbled
1 tablespoon minced fresh chives
Freshly ground black pepper
6 strips bacon, preferably thick country-style

1. Mix the brown sugar, herbs, and a generous amount of pepper in a medium shallow bowl and combine thoroughly. Coat the bacon strips, one at a time, by dipping the

raw bacon into the bowl of spices and coating well on both sides. You may need to use your hands to press the mixture onto the bacon so it adheres well.

2. Preheat the broiler. Lay the bacon on the rack of a broiler pan and place under the broiler for 1 to 3 minutes, with the oven door slightly ajar, or until the bacon looks cooked and is bubbling and glazed. Turn the broiler pan once while it's cooking to ensure even browning. Watch the bacon carefully to make sure it doesn't burn.

3. Very carefully, using tongs, flip the bacon over and broil for 1 to 2 minutes more, turning the pan halfway through the cooking time. The bacon is ready when it's cooked and the glaze is bubbling. Let cool for 30 seconds before serving; it will be very hot.

CORNED BEEF HASH

SERVES 3 TO 4

This breakfast classic is straightforward comfort food. It's traditionally made around St. Patrick's Day, when many cooks have leftover corned beef. If you don't have corned beef sitting around in your refrigerator, be sure to ask your deli to slice the corned beef about ½ inch thick for you. If you have leftover cooked potatoes (boiled or roasted), you can put this together in a matter of minutes.

Serve topped with poached eggs (see page 53), accompanied by toast, English muffins, biscuits, or crunchy bread.

INGREDIENTS

1 cup peeled and quartered potatoes (8 ounces)

2 tablespoons olive oil

1 cup packed chopped onion (about 1 large)

1 tablespoon chopped fresh thyme or 1 teaspoon dried and crumbled

Salt

Freshly ground black pepper

8 ounces cooked corned beef, cut into ½-inch slices and then cubed (1½ cups)

2 tablespoons finely chopped fresh parsley

1. Place the potatoes in a large saucepan and cover with cold water. Bring to a boil over high heat, reduce the heat, and cook for about 10 minutes, or until almost tender, but not falling apart. Drain and cool. Cut the potatoes into cubes the same size as the corned beef. Alternately, cut leftover cooked potatoes into cubes.

2. In a 9- to 10-inch skillet, heat 1 tablespoon of the oil over low heat. Add the onion, half of the thyme, and season with salt and pepper and cook for 10 minutes, stirring frequently, until the onion is a pale golden color. Raise the heat to medium and add the remaining oil, the cooked potatoes, corned beef, and remaining thyme; flatten the mixture out into the skillet with a metal spatula to create a thick pancake-like layer. Cook *undisturbed* for 5 minutes. Using the spatula, carefully flip the mixture over like a big pancake (don't worry if it doesn't hold together perfectly). If the skillet seems dry, add another ½ to 1 tablespoon oil. Cook *undisturbed* for 5 minutes more; check the underside of the hash to make sure it's turned a light brown color. Turn off the heat and sprinkle the parsley onto the finished hash.

3. Divide the hash between three or four plates and serve hot.

CHORIZO HASH

SERVES 4

This is a full-flavored hash—combining buttery potatoes, spicy chorizo sausage, and caramelized onions. Serve the hash with poached (see page 53), fried, or scrambled (see page 44) eggs. It also makes a great side dish to omelets (page 55), pancakes (page 90), or French toast (page 102).

INGREDIENTS

1 tablespoon olive or vegetable oil

1 medium onion, chopped

1 tablespoon chopped fresh thyme or 1 teaspoon dried

Salt

Freshly ground black pepper

8 ounces chorizo sausage

1 large potato (about 13 ounces), like Yukon Gold, peeled and cut into 1-inch cubes

Hot pepper sauce

1. In a large, heavy skillet, heat the oil over low heat. Add the onion and half of the thyme, season with salt and pepper and cook, stirring frequently, for about 10 minutes, or until the onion is pale golden brown and tender.

2. Meanwhile, use a sharp knife to cut the casing that contains the sausage. Remove the sausage meat (discard the casing) and crumble into the skillet with the onion. Cook for 2 minutes, stirring well.

Raise the heat to medium and add the potato, remaining thyme, and another dash of salt and pepper. Cook, stirring occasionally, for about 15 minutes. Add a dash of hot pepper sauce and cook for another 5 to 10 minutes, or until the potatoes are tender and the sausage meat is thoroughly cooked.

3. Serve hot alongside eggs.

FLAVORED CREAM CHEESE: TRANSFORM YOUR BAGEL

QUICK AND SIMPLE 🕐

We love whipping cream cheese with various flavorings and spices. The basic recipe follows, but have fun coming up with your own variations. Serve flavored cream cheese with bagels, scones (page 22), toast, baguettes, muffins (page 17, page 19, page 21, and page 24) or use as an omelet filling (page 55).

Mix 1 cup whipped cream cheese, at room temperature, with any of the following ingredients. The flavored cream cheese will keep, covered and refrigerated, for about 5 days.

TRIPLE LEMON CREAM CHEESE

1½ tablespoons freshly squeezed lemon juice, 1 teaspoon grated lemon zest, 1 tablespoon chopped fresh lemon verbena or lemon thyme, and 2 finely chopped scallions. Also try this with lime juice, lime zest, and chives.

TRIPLE OLIVE–SCALLION CREAM CHEESE

¼ cup finely or coarsely chopped pitted black olives, ¼ cup chopped pitted green olives, and ¼ cup chopped pimiento-stuffed green olives with 1 finely chopped scallion, and salt and pepper to taste.

ROASTED GARLIC AND HERB CREAM CHEESE

8 garlic cloves, drizzled with 1 tablespoon olive oil and a sprinkling of freshly ground black pepper roasted in a 350 degree F oven for 15 minutes, cooled, and chopped; 1 tablespoon chopped fresh thyme, basil, and/or rosemary.

ARTICHOKE HEART AND ROASTED RED PEPPER CREAM CHEESE

⅓ cup chopped cooked artichoke hearts (if using jarred or bottled, drain and rinse before using), ¼ cup chopped roasted red pepper, and salt and freshly ground pepper to taste.

CARROT-RADISH-PARSLEY CREAM CHEESE

⅓ cup grated raw carrot, ¼ cup grated raw radish, ¼ cup finely chopped fresh parsley, and salt and freshly ground black pepper to taste. You could also add ¼ cup raisins or dried cranberries.

Continued…

...continued

GREEN CREAM CHEESE

2 finely chopped scallions, ¼ cup finely chopped fresh parsley, 2 tablespoons drained capers, and 1 tablespoon minced fresh chives.

TOMATO-HORSERADISH

½ cup finely chopped fresh ripe tomatoes, 1½ tablespoons drained horseradish, and salt and freshly ground black pepper to taste.

SOUTHERN PECAN CREAM CHEESE

½ cup pecans, lightly toasted in a 350 degree F oven for 10 minutes, coarsely chopped; 2 tablespoons honey; and a dash of allspice.

PEPPER CREAM CHEESE

⅓ cup pepper jelly, heated until thin, and a dash of hot pepper sauce.

MAPLE-GINGER CREAM CHEESE

¼ cup maple syrup and ¼ cup slivered candied ginger.

NEW ENGLAND CREAM CHEESE

¼ cup maple syrup; ¼ cup coarsely chopped wild Maine blueberries or regular blueberries, and ¼ cup blueberry jam, heated slightly until thin.

LEMON-HERB BUTTER

MAKES ABOUT ½ CUP | QUICK AND SIMPLE 🕐

We made this fragrant butter to go with the Basil and Goat Cheese Muffins (page 21), but it's also a great accompaniment to the Crêpes (page 97), or drizzled on top of the Eggs Baked in Pancetta Cups (page 48). It's delicious spread on scones, toast, or egg sandwiches.

INGREDIENTS

½ stick (¼ cup) unsalted butter, at room temperature

1 tablespoon chopped fresh thyme or 1 teaspoon dried and crumbled

1 tablespoon minced fresh chives

1½ teaspoons grated lemon zest

Freshly ground black pepper

In a small bowl, cream the butter with a soft spatula. Add the thyme, chives, zest, and a generous grinding of pepper and mix well. Cover and refrigerate until needed. The butter will last for 48 hours, or you can freeze it (see page 128).

PEACH-GINGER BUTTER AND OTHER FRUIT BUTTERS

MAKES ABOUT ¾ CUP BUTTER | QUICK AND SIMPLE 🕐

Serve these fruit-filled butters with muffins (page 17), toast, scones (page 22), and biscuits, or place a small dollop on top of pancakes (page 90), French toast (page 102), and waffles (page 105).

Fruit butter will keep, covered and refrigerated, for several days. You can also place the butter on a sheet of plastic wrap, roll it into a log shape, and freeze for several months.

INGREDIENTS

1 cup ripe peeled and thinly sliced peaches or any other fruit (peeled and stemmed if necessary)

½ stick (¼ cup) unsalted butter, at room temperature

2 tablespoons chopped crystallized ginger or ½ teaspoon spice (such as cinnamon, cardamom, nutmeg, allspice, lemon basil, lemon verbena, etc.)

1. Place the peaches in the container of a food processor or blender and whirl until blended. You can keep the fruit chunky or puree it until smooth.

2. Place the butter in a small bowl and cream it with a soft spatula. Add the peaches and the ginger and stir until well incorporated. Place into a small ramekin or bowl and chill for at least 30 minutes before serving. The butter will last for 48 hours.

VARIATIONS

Jam Butter: Cream 1 stick unsalted butter with ¼ cup of your favorite jam

Apple-Cinnamon-Honey: Cream ½ cup applesauce with ¼ cup butter, ⅛ teaspoon cinnamon, ⅛ teaspoon allspice, and 2 tablespoons honey

Pear-Ginger-Allspice: Cream ½ cup pear butter or pear jelly with ¼ cup butter, ⅛ teaspoon each powdered ginger and allspice, and 1 tablespoon chopped crystallized ginger

Blueberry–Maple Syrup: Cream 1 cup whole or pureed blueberries with ¼ cup butter and 2 tablespoons maple syrup

Raspberry–Fresh Mint: Cream 1 cup pureed raspberries with ¼ cup butter and 1½ tablespoons finely chopped fresh mint

Fig and Lemon Zest: Cream 1 cup fresh figs, stemmed and pureed, with ¼ cup butter and 1 tablespoon lemon zest

8

CHAPTER

DRINKS

THICK DOUBLE-CHOCOLATE COCOA

SERVES 1 TO 2

There's nothing like a thick, steaming hot cup of cocoa to make breakfast taste like a celebration. There is cocoa and then there's *cocoa*—trust us when we tell you this one is something special. A rich combination of dark and milk chocolate mixed with milk and cream, the cocoa is topped with a light dusting of ground cinnamon and chile powder. The chile and cinnamon add great dimension to the chocolate flavors. Serve it simple or top with whipped cream and marshmallows!

INGREDIENTS

1 ounce dark chocolate, chopped

1 ounce milk chocolate, chopped

⅔ cup low-fat or regular milk

⅓ cup heavy cream

About 1½ teaspoons sugar

Dash of ground cinnamon (optional)

Dash of mild red chile powder (optional)

1. Add the dark and milk chocolates to a medium saucepan set over *very* low heat. Use a soft spatula to stir the chocolate until thoroughly melted.

2. In another saucepan, heat the milk and cream over low heat until hot. Slowly add the warm milk mixture to the melted chocolate, while whisking, to create a smooth cocoa mixture. Add the sugar to taste.

3. Pour the cocoa into 1 or 2 mugs (it's pretty rich stuff) and sprinkle very lightly with the cinnamon and chile powder, if desired.

STONEWALL BLOODYS

SERVES 2 TO 4

Bloody Marys have become the cliché drink of brunch. But sometimes clichés can be a good choice, particularly when the drink is a good, spicy one. We use vegetable juice spiked with a generous dash of horseradish, hot pepper sauce, Worcestershire sauce, and spices. You can serve this as a Virgin Bloody or mix in vodka and sit back and enjoy the morning! Although you can serve the drink with the traditional celery stick, we like to add a cucumber spear or a New England touch—a dilly bean!

INGREDIENTS

2 cups vegetable juice or tomato juice

1½ tablespoons horseradish, drained

1 tablespoon freshly squeezed lemon juice

1½ teaspoons Worcestershire sauce

Sea salt

Freshly ground black pepper

Dash of hot pepper sauce

1 cup ice cubes

4 to 6 ounces vodka

2 to 4 dilly beans or pickled martini onions (see Note)

1. In a drink shaker or large pitcher, combine the vegetable juice, horseradish, lemon juice, Worcestershire, salt and pepper to taste, hot pepper sauce, and ice cubes. Shake vigorously.

2. Add the vodka (4 ounces makes a good drink but 6 ounces will really wake you up) and shake again. Serve with ice cubes or strain the drinks into 2 to 4 glasses, and place a dilly bean or two in the middle of each.

NOTE
Dilly beans are green beans pickled with dill, garlic, and often chile peppers. They can be found in specialty food shops and at farmers' markets.

VARIATIONS
Instead of dilly beans, serve with:

* seedless English cucumbers cut into thin, long wedges

* a skewer with a small cube of Italian cheese, salami, and a pickled pepper (like a pepperoncini), laid across the top of the glass

BLOOD ORANGE MIMOSAS

SERVES 2

What better way to celebrate a Sunday morning or holiday brunch than a combination of Champagne and freshly squeezed orange juice, preferably from blood oranges? This recipe serves two and can easily be multiplied.

INGREDIENTS

1 cup Champagne, chilled

¼ cup freshly squeezed orange juice or blood orange juice, chilled

1 tablespoon Grand Marnier or Cointreau

2 thin strips orange peel

Divide the Champagne between two Champagne or martini glasses. Add the orange juice and Grand Marnier and gently stir. Loop the orange strips across the edge of the glasses. Serve cold.

STONEWALL KITCHEN
BREAKFAST MENUS

Relaxed Sunday Brunch with Friends

BERRY SALAD WITH MINT SYRUP
(page 30)

CRUSTLESS BREAKFAST QUICHE *(page 61)*

BLINTZES TWO WAYS *(page 100)*

BLOOD ORANGE–GLAZED
SAUSAGES *(page 113)*

CHILE POWDER AND BROWN SUGAR–
GLAZED BACON *(page 117)*

BLOOD ORANGE MIMOSAS *(page 136)*

Gotta' Run Monday

BREAKFAST FRUIT SMOOTHIES *(page 33)*

PERFECTLY GOOD GRANOLA BARS *(page 40)*

Weekend Breakfast with the Kids

THICK DOUBLE-CHOCOLATE
COCOA *(page 133)*

BREAKFAST FRUIT SMOOTHIES *(page 33)*

WALNUT PANCAKES WITH
MAPLE-GLAZED APPLES *(page 95)*

CHOCOLATE WAFFLES WITH
CHOCOLATE-MAPLE SAUCE
(page 105)

MAPLE-GLAZED BACON *(page 117)*

Breakfast in Bed

BLOOD ORANGE MIMOSAS *(page 136)*

LOBSTER BENEDICT WITH MEYER LEMON–
SCALLION BUTTER *(page 65)*

BASIL AND GOAT CHEESE MUFFINS *(page 21)*

LEMON-HERB BUTTER *(page 127)*

BERRY SALAD WITH MINT SYRUP *(page 30)*
AND BUTTER COOKIES

Sunday Morning with the Family and the Paper

THICK DOUBLE-CHOCOLATE
COCOA *(page 133)*

ESPRESSO

BREAKFAST PIZZA *(page 84)*

BERRY SALAD WITH MINT SYRUP *(page 30)*

Healthy Morning

BREAKFAST FRUIT SMOOTHIES *(page 33)*

BERRY SALAD WITH MINT SYRUP *(page 30)*

GOOD-FOR-YOU WHOLE-GRAIN BLUEBERRY
PANCAKES *(page 93)*

TURKEY AND SAGE SAUSAGE
PATTIES *(page 115)*

Summer Breakfast on the Patio

BREAKFAST CORN FRITTERS *(page 89)*

SPINACH, FETA, AND TOMATO
FRITTATA *(page 58)*

PAN-FRIED BREAKFAST TOMATOES
AND ZUCCHINI *(page 110)*
or
SPANISH TOMATO TOAST WITH CHEESE
AND BASIL *(page 75)*

PEACH, SOUR CREAM, AND CRYSTALLIZED
GINGER MUFFINS *(page 19)*

PEACH-GINGER BUTTER *(page 128)*

ICED TEA WITH FRESH MINT AND LEMON
VERBENA LEAVES AND ICED COFFEE

Mediterranean Breakfast

PROVENÇAL-STYLE BAKED EGGS *(page 51)*

PAN-FRIED BREAKFAST TOMATOES
AND ZUCCHINI *(page 110)*

SPANISH TOMATO TOAST WITH CHEESE
AND BASIL *(page 75)*

MEDITERRANEAN YOGURT BAR *(page 32)*

CRUSTY BREAD AND OLIVE OIL

LEMON-HERB BUTTER *(page 127)*

ESPRESSO AND CAPPUCCINO

New York Wake Up

NEW YORK–STYLE SMOKED SALMON
SCRAMBLE *(page 44)*

SILVER DOLLAR POTATO PANCAKES *(page 90)*

BAGELS

ASSORTED FLAVORED CREAM
CHEESES *(page 124)*

COFFEE

Do-Ahead Brunch Party

STONEWALL BLOODYS *(page 134)*

BERRY SALAD WITH MINT SYRUP *(page 30)*

BLINTZES TWO WAYS *(page 100)*

OPEN-FACED BREAKFAST SANDWICH WITH
PEQUILLO PEPPERS *(page 76)*

B.E.L.T.S *(page 79)*, CUT INTO QUARTERS

GLAZED BACON THREE WAYS *(page 117)*

Holiday Brunch

STONEWALL BLOODYS *(page 134)*

BLOOD ORANGE MIMOSAS *(page 136)*

COCONUT-ORANGE-PECAN COFFEE
CAKE *(page 26)*

SMOKED SALMON AND ARUGULA
BENEDICT WITH ARUGULA-LEMON
BUTTER *(page 68)*

BREAKFAST SALAD WITH BACON, FRIED
EGGS, AND CROÛTES *(page 81)*

APPLE AND APRICOT BUTTERMILK SCONES
WITH MAPLE-ALMOND GLAZE *(page 22)*

ASSORTMENT OF FRUIT BUTTERS *(page 128)*
and FLAVORED CREAM CHEESES *(page 124)*

THICK DOUBLE-CHOCOLATE
COCOA *(page 133)*

INDEX

Index

TABLE OF EQUIVALENTS

The exact equivalents in the following tables have been rounded for convenience.

LIQUID/DRY MEASUREMENTS

U.S.	METRIC
¼ teaspoon	1.25 milliliters
½ teaspoon	2.5 milliliters
1 teaspoon	5 milliliters
1 tablespoon (3 teaspoons)	15 milliliters
1 fluid ounce (2 tablespoons)	30 milliliters
¼ cup	60 milliliters
⅓ cup	80 milliliters
½ cup	120 milliliters
1 cup	240 milliliters
1 pint (2 cups)	480 milliliters
1 quart (4 cups, 32 ounces)	960 milliliters
1 gallon (4 quarts)	3.84 liters
1 ounce (by weight)	28 grams
1 pound	448 grams
2.2 pounds	1 kilogram

LENGTHS

U.S.	METRIC
⅛ inch	3 millimeters
¼ inch	6 millimeters
½ inch	12 millimeters
1 inch	2.5 centimeters

OVEN TEMPERATURE

FAHRENHEIT	CELSIUS	GAS
250	120	½
275	140	1
300	150	2
325	160	3
350	180	4
375	190	5
400	200	6
425	220	7
450	230	8
475	240	9
500	260	10